STEP UP TO THE PLATE

Baseball, Judaism & How to
Win the Game of Life

STEP UP TO THE PLATE

Baseball, Judaism & How to
Win the Game of Life

Rabbi Yisroel Roll

A Targum Press Book

Published and distributed by:
TARGUM PRESS, INC.
22700 W. Eleven Mile Rd.
Southfield, MI 48034
E-mail: targum@targum.com
Fax: 888-298-9992
www.targum.com

Distributed by:
FELDHEIM PUBLISHERS
208 Airport Executive Park
Nanuet, NY 10954

Printed in Israel by Chish

Rabbi CHAIM P. SCHEINBERG
Rosh Hayeshiva "TORAH ORE"
and Morah Hora'ah of Kiryat Mattersdorf

הרב חיים פינחס שיינברג
ראש ישיבת "תורה אור"
ומורה הוראה דקרית מטרסדורף

ט"ו באב התשס"ט
August 5, 2009

מכתב ברכה

Twenty years ago, Yisroel Roll and his wife came to visit me in my home in *Yerushalayim* and asked me whether he should leave the security of his law practice in Toronto to follow his dream of learning for *Smicha* in *Eretz Yisroel*. Yisroel raised his hand upward in the form of a question and asked me if he had the right to jeopardize his wife's "security" by leaving a thriving law practice and exchanging it for a much more modest lifestyle as a *kollel* student. I gently slapped his hand and said: "Torah is security!"

I am gratified that Yisroel heeded my **advice** and left law to come to *Eretz Yisroel* to learn. Since then he has served as a Rov in London, England, founded the UK Encounter Kiruv Conference and has written various books on Torah and Psychology. He has visited me many times in my apartment to keep me up to date, advise with me and has also brought his Summer Seminary Experience groups to visit with me to receive *Divrei Bracha* and *Chizuk*.

On his most recent visit he brought me his new manuscript, *Stepping Up to the Plate-Baseball, Judaism and Winning the Game of Life*, which is an inspiring introduction to *hashkafas HaTorah* and will hopefully open the hearts of all who are looking to come closer to *Hakadosh Baruch Hu*.

I would like to convey my heartfelt *brachah* to Reb Yisroel, that through his *kiruv* activities, he should continue to inspire *Acheinu Bnei Yisroel* on their journey back home תחת כנפי השכינה להרבות כבוד שמים

רחוב פנים מאירות 2, ירושלים, ת.ד. 6979, טל. 537–1513 (02), ישראל
2 Panim Meirot St., Jerusalem, P.O.B. 6979, Tel. (02) 537-1513, Israel

OHR SOMAYACH אור שמחה
TANENBAUM COLLEGE

August 26, 2009

Rabbi Yisroel Roll possesses unique gifts of human sensitivity, understanding of Torah philosophy, and the ability to communicate clearly and effectively in writing. His books are products of these gifts, and they fill an essential place in Torah literature.

He combines intimate understanding of contemporary life — its challenges, pitfalls, inspirations and temptations — with Torah sources that point the way to reaching maximum spiritual development even within that life setting. The popularity of his books shows that he is serving a widespread need for Torah sources of spiritual guidance.

One reason for his success is the consistency between what he writes and who he is — *tocho k'varo* — he lives what he preaches. "*Words that come from the heart penetrate the heart.*" I offer him my *berachah* that he should be successful in all his endeavors to bring the Jewish people closer to the Creator.

Rabbi Dr Dovid Gottlieb
Yeshivat Ohr Somayach

Jerusalem • New York • Detroit
Chicago • Miami • Toronto
Montreal • London • Johannesburg
Cape Town • Sydney

GLORIA MARTIN CAMPUS
1 Ohr Somayach Street
22 Shimon Hatzadik Street
POB 18103, Ma'alot Daphna
Jerusalem 91180 Israel
Tel: 02-581-0315 Fax: 02-581-2890
Email: office@ohr.edu

OHR SOMAYACH INTERNATIONAL
1399 Coney Island Avenue
Brooklyn, NY 11230
Tel: 718-677-6200 Fax: 718-677-6299
Email: ny@ohr.edu

CANADIAN FRIENDS OF OHR SOMAYACH
446 Spadina Road, Suite 203
Toronto, Ontario M5P-3M2
Tel: 416-483-4683 Fax: 416-483-6712
Email: office: info@foresthilljewishcentre.com

For my father,

Walter Roll, z"l,

Who made the time to pitch
around with me,
cheered me at my
Little League games,
and taught me to how to
hit life's curveballs

This book is dedicated

to the memory of

יצחק בן יעקב ז"ל

העניל העלדא בת העניך מרדכי ז"ל

Cyril and Hazel Symons, *z"l*

Dedicated by their son,

Jonathan Symons
London, England

Contents

Preface

I grew up playing Little League Baseball in a small suburb north of Montreal called Chomedey, in the city of Laval. We played ball for the Laval Little League at the scruffy dirt diamond of Kennedy Park — which we thought was Yankee Stadium. I was a pretty good pitcher and my French-Canadian friend, Francois, was my talented catcher. A neat little one-two package, Francois and I worked our way through the T-Ball league, then Pee Wee, minors, and then, as seasoned veterans at the ripe old age of twelve, we made it to the big time — the majors. Our local team was the Tigers, and we were elated when we won our local division championship. But that was only half the story.

Our coveted goal was to make the All-Star team. That year, Francois and I achieved our dream: we were both picked by coach Norman Gurevitch to join the Laval Little League All-Star team. That the Tigers won our local division title was small stuff compared to representing the Laval Little League in inter-city competition. We dreamed of making it all the way to Williamsport, Pennsylvania, to the Little League World Series.

xii ■ STEP UP TO THE PLATE

At our first practice the coach called all of us together. "Boys," he said, "this summer, this whistle is your boss. You hear it and you hustle — or you don't start on opening day." This coach meant business. I was here to learn about the finer art of baseball — and about the whistle, our new boss.

That season I learned that baseball was a metaphor for life. "Look alive," said the coach. "Keep your head in the game." From that I learned that focus and concentration in all areas of life were the keys to success. "Hustle down the base path" meant you had to take the initiative and think one step ahead in order to make it in life. And I learned the most difficult yet most important lesson of life: *You are going to strike out...and when you do, don't throw down your bat. Don't give up, and don't lose your cool. Put your baseball glove on and get back in the field. Look forward to the next inning. You'll get a hit next time up. Or you won't. But you have to keep your head up and keep going.*

I have had to remember that message every day of my life.

My All-Star game debut came later that season when I was chosen as the starting pitcher for our interleague championship game against the Campeau League All-Stars. I pitched our team to an 11-3 victory — it still stands out in my mind as one of the highlights of my youth.

My baseball career went on hold after that as I began to get into youth activities and high school. Three years later, when I was fifteen, I spent a summer in Israel on a high school trip with the ninth-grade class of Herzliah High School. We spent the summer touring through the mountains, caves, tunnels, and rivers of Jewish history. I was so inspired during the trip that I wrote my parents a letter informing them that from then on I was going to be more observant. As I grew older and began to study and live Jewishly, I discovered that the lessons and guidance for life that can be found in Jewish thought have an uncanny correlation with the lessons I learned on the baseball diamond. And that is how this book came to be.

Baseball is our national pastime. It evokes passion and teaches us about life. So does Judaism — not the once-a-year Judaism that some of us suffer through during the High Holidays, but the vibrant Judaism that guides, nurtures, and inspires, the Judaism I have come to know and live. Real Judaism is not a religion, but a way of thinking, a way of approaching and getting the most out of life. It is actually a system designed for self-actualization and growth. Judaism encourages each of us to "step up to the plate" by becoming aware of our personal strengths and qualities. When we get in touch with our sense of self, then we can discover our life mission by matching our strengths and interests to our life circumstances. Stepping up to the plate means that we are empowered to take a swing, to take a shot at achieving the goals of our lives by getting on base and scoring a run.

In this book, we will use the baseball model that is so familiar to us to gain the confidence to stand with resolve in the batter's box; face life's curveballs, sinkers, and knuckle balls; and "take a cut." Both baseball and the game of life are won and lost with concentration, focus, and knowing where you are on the field or on base. To win the opportunity called life, you have to keep your head about you and "in the game."

This book is about learning how to develop a belief in ourselves so we can meet life's challenges and get onto the spiritual "base paths"— the soul of real Jewish living. It is no fun getting called out on strikes. But even if we swing and strike out, I consider that success, only because we believed we could get a hit. Believing is winning. In this way, we will discover that Judaism is actually a system for living successful lives and can help us win the game of life.

Acknowledgments

I would like to express my heartfelt gratitude to the following individuals who have made significant contributions to the development of this project:

My good friend, Jonathan Symons of London, for his friendship and support. Your character and values of *chesed*, compassion for the less fortunate, and dedication to the cause of building the Jewish people are examples of your "sportsman-like conduct" which have earned you a "good name" in the Jewish Hall of Fame, as the *Ethics of the Fathers* states, "The crown of a good name surpasses them all" (4:17). Since your name is Yehudah, my *berachah* to you is that you continue to work for the Jewish people so that through your efforts and the efforts of those like you, "He will raise a banner for the nations and assemble the castaways of Israel; and he will gather in the dispersed ones of Yehudah from the four corners of the earth" (Isaiah 11:12).

Rabbi Noach Weinberg, *zt"l*, founder of Aish HaTorah, whose *shiur* and essay "The Five Levels of Pleasure" form the basis for the concept of relative values of singles, doubles, triples, and home runs as a system for motivation in life described in this book. My blessing is to the students of Rabbi Noach around the world: May you continue to be inspired by your rebbe's words and teachings, as the *navi* Ezra says, "We are the servants of God of Heaven and earth, and we are rebuilding a temple that had been built these many years ago; a great king of Israel built it and laid its foundation" (Ezra 5:11).

My rebbe, Rabbi Dovid Gottlieb of Jerusalem, who reviewed the manuscript as he does all my work and for his insights and amendments, which have greatly enhanced the book. You have taken a genuine interest in my development and have served as my guide and mentor. My *berachah* to you is "*Chizku v'imtzu* — Be strong and courageous" (Deuteronomy 31:6) by developing the strength and courage in all your *talmidim* in their *avodas Hashem*.

Rabbi Shimon Apisdorf of Baltimore, who collaborated extensively with me on the concepts and development of this book. You are one of the most visionary and creative writers on the Jewish scene today, and my *berachah* to you is that all your writings shall be like those of Shmuel HaNavi, about whom it is written, "*Vayichtov basefer vayanach lifnei Hashem* — And he wrote it in a book and placed it before Hashem" (Samuel I 10:25).

Rabbi Dovid Orlofsky of Jerusalem, for the time and effort he invested in reviewing with me ideas and concepts in the manuscript and for sharing with me inspiring insights that I have incorporated in the book. You are one of the foremost motivational speakers in the Torah world, and my *berachah* to you is that your *divrei chizuk* and Torah should be, in the words of the *navi* Yirmeyahu, "*Vehayah b'libi k'eish bo'eres* — His word would be like a burning fire in my heart" (Jeremiah 20:9), and may your words ignite the souls of all of your *talmidim*.

Rabbi Zalman Nissel of Baltimore, who spent many hours reviewing the manuscript and shared with me invaluable insights that have greatly enhanced the book. Reb Zalman is an *askan* of great integrity and energy in the Baltimore community who has been instrumental in enhancing the lives of many people. My *berachah* to you is that your building of lives in the community shall provide *chizuk* for many, so that they shall say, "*Ki hayisa ezrasah li, u'v'tzel kenafecha aranen* — For You have been a help for me; in the shelter of Your wings I joyously sing" (Psalms 63:8).

Gary and Ellen Davis of Greenwich, Connecticut, for their support and investment in my projects and programs. You are visionary community activists who have helped build communities and lives around the world, and my blessing to you is that all your projects should be based on the words of the prophet, "And I will build for Him a faithful house" (Samuel I 2:35).

Gary Torgow of Detroit, for his ongoing friendship and support. From our days together in yeshivah, you took me under your wing and taught me how to inspire others, and your advice has guided my every endeavor. You are much more than an *askan* — you are an *eved Hashem* who has genuine compassion for all who turn to you. May you continue to be a leader in your efforts to build lives and *klal Yisrael*. May Hashem bless you with the words of the *navi*, "*Bayom hahu yihiyeh Hashem tzevakos la'ateres tzvi v'litzefiras tifarah lishe'ar amo* — On that day, Hashem, Master of legions, will be a crown of delight for the remnant of His people" (Isaiah 28:5).

Dr. Yisroel and Robin Ingber of Toronto, for their friendship, support, and gracious *hachnasas orchim*. You are building a wonderful Torah family based on *middos tovos* and *ahavas Torah*, and my *berachah* to you is in the words of the *navi*: "Behold, I am building a house for the Name of Hashem my God, to sanctify Him" (Chronicles II 2:3).

Rabbi Shimon Kurland for his friendship, loyalty, and support. Rabbi Kurland, you are a true *chaver* who has shown selfless dedication and assistance to me and my family. You are a visionary *mechanech* who has founded the *Darchei Binah, Chochmas Lev, and Afikei Torah* seminaries on the principles of *komemius* — building the *neshamos* and *middos* of your *talmidos*. You and your rebbetzin have only the best interests of your *talmidos* at heart and in mind, and my *berachah* to you is, in the words of David HaMelech: "*Pakadeta ha'aretz vateshokekeha rabbas tashrena peleg Elokim malei mayim tachin deganam ki chen techineha; telameiha ravei nacheis gedudeiha birvivim temogegenah tzimchah tevarech* — You paid heed to the earth and watered it, You enriched it abundantly with Hashem's stream filled with water; You prepare their grain, for thus do you prepare it, to abundantly water its ridges, settle its furrows, with showers you soften it, You bless its growth" (*Tehillim* 65: 10–11).

My brother-in-law, Rabbi Menachem Nissel of Jerusalem, for the ongoing kindness and support he has shown to my family. Even though you are a world-renowned speaker and *mashpia*, in your humility you always find the time to give personal *chizuk* to your *talmidim*. My *berachah* to you, in the words of the *navi*: "*Vayechazkem la'avodas beis Hashem* — And he encouraged them in the service of the House of Hashem" (ibid. 35:2).

My editor, Debbie Ismailoff, and the other members of the Targum Press staff — Bassi Gruen, Esther Heller, Allison Fried, Beena Sklare, and Aryeh Mahr — for your professionalism and attention to detail. My *berachah* to you is that about all your work it will be said, "You shall inscribe on the stones all the words of this Torah, well clarified" (Deuteronomy 27:8).

My children, Rivka, Avrami, Dovid Simcha, Rina, Yehudah, and Channah, for your *hislahavus*, energy, and *simchas hachaim*. You have added so much joy and inspiration to our lives. Mommy joins me in giving you this *berachah*: "*Va'asu lachem lev chadash v'ruach chadashah* — And make for yourselves a new heart and a new spirit" (Ezekiel 18:31).

My wife, Julie, for standing by my side and for believing in me. I am privileged to have you as my life partner as we travel together on the base paths of life. May the words of Shlomo HaMelech be ever-present in your life: "*Kol dodi hinei zeh ba, medaleg al heharim, mekapetz al hageva'os* — The voice of my Beloved! Behold, it came suddenly to redeem me, as if leaping over mountains, skipping over hills" (Song of Songs 2:8).

Chapter One
Buying a Glove

While on a state visit to India in 1997, John Major, then prime minister of Britain, went to visit an ancient tribe that inhabits the mountain range between India and Tibet. He attended a poignant coming-of-age ceremony in which a group of thirteen-year-old boys was being welcomed as men into the tribe. The prime minister watched as the father of each boy walked up to his son and presented him with a symbol of manhood and tribal identity — a Kalashnikov rifle.

This ceremony speaks volumes about the values of that society, highlighting their most important value — self-preservation amidst the warring mountain tribes and communal pride in taking part in the tribe's defense.

During Passover of 1999, I, too, experienced a coming-of-age ceremony, American style. My family and I were spending Passover with my in-laws in Memphis, Tennessee, and my parents flew to Memphis from Montreal to spend the holidays with us. Since we lived in England then, that was literally the first time my kids were able to be with both sets of grandparents simultaneously. (So let's not take those routine family visits for granted.)

While we were in Memphis I took my son, who was then nine, and my dad to a sporting goods store so that my dad could advise me on the purchase of my son's first baseball glove. In England, we played only soccer and cricket.

There we were, in the middle of the baseball section, trying on baseball mitts and throwing baseballs to each other in the aisle to make sure the glove was a good fit and the ball would go easily into the pocket of the glove.

"This is the one," my dad said finally, "and I'm paying," he added, beaming with pride. I was happy to let my dad pay; I felt like I was experiencing the continuity of a family tradition. My grandfather had bought me my first glove, and now my dad was doing the same for my son.

While trying on gloves in the store, I had flashbacks of my dad and me pitching a baseball in our Montreal backyard and my dad throwing me practice fly balls and giving me pointers on how to backpedal when the ball was behind me. I remembered how he took me to my Little League games and cheered me from the stands. My father taught me how to play as my father's father had taught him. And now my dad was literally handing down this tradition to my son.

That was a moment of spirituality. In it I captured a taste of immortality. If my son passes on the tradition to his son, then I could live forever, so to speak. For my son, it didn't mean that much...another sport to be added to the list of badminton, soccer, and cricket. But I bet he will recall the event with fondness when I accompany him and his son to the baseball store in thirty years' time. Only then will his own visit to buy his first glove take on real meaning for him.

What are the values that I am instilling in my kids? What do I hold dear that I would like to see continued into the next generation? Is it an appreciation for the finer things in life — good wine, good food, my love of baseball? Maybe it's expertise at chess or the right way to wash your car. What are the things that I can't touch or see but are the most valuable concepts and morals I can transmit to my children? If I could put my finger on them, wouldn't that be nothing less than figuring out what life is all about?

At the Passover Seder the most prevalent number that we come across in the text and throughout the customs of the evening is the number four. There are four questions of the *Mah Nishtanah*, we drink four cups of wine, and we discuss the four sons. Why the number four? The answer is that at the end of the Seder, we sing a famous song called "Who Knows One?" One of the lines in the song goes "Who knows four? Four are our matriarchs" — Sarah, Rebecca, Rachel, and Leah. These matriarchs are the founding mothers of the Jewish people. Sarah founded the belief in one God with Abraham, and they had a son Issac. Isaac carried on the traditions of his parents and married Rebecca, who had Jacob. And Jacob married Rachel and Leah, who gave birth to the twelve tribes.

These four founding mothers gave birth to the Jewish people. The main theme of the Passover Seder is the birth of the Jewish nation as it went from slavery in Egypt to the Exodus and religious freedom. So we use the number four throughout the Passover Seder as representative of the four matriarchs. Thus, motherhood and the birth of the Jewish nation through the four matriarchs is the symbolic theme of the Passover Seder.

Even Jews who are estranged from Jewish life have a craving to be at a Seder. Passover awakens a need in them for spiritual connection to their people. At the Seder we convey the love of our heritage to the next generation. We express that love not only verbally, but experientially. We show our children and feel with them the bitterness of the *maror*, or bitter herbs, and the salty tears of slavery. We taste the wine of freedom and the crops of springtime and rejuvenation. We bridge the generation gap by experiencing Judaism with our children.

During *Maggid*, the narrative section of the Haggadah, we respond to the children's questions in *Mah Nishtanah* by saying: "It is a mitzvah for us to tell about the miracles that happened when the Jews left Egypt. The more someone tells about it, the more he deserves to be praised."

Rabbi Shalom Noach Brozofsky, the author of *Nesivos Shalom*, asks, Why do we expound upon the miracles of going out of Egypt? Why is it more praiseworthy to elaborate specifically upon the wonders that God did for us there? It is not considered more praiseworthy to blow the shofar an extra one hundred times on Rosh HaShanah. It is not considered more praiseworthy to fast an extra hour on Yom Kippur. It is not considered more praiseworthy to light extra candles on Chanukah. So why is it considered praiseworthy to talk all night about the miracles of our exodus from Egypt? No other aspect of Judaism has this concept of doing more than the required amount. So why is doing extra applicable on Passover?

Rabbi Brozofsky answers: The Passover Seder is the Rosh HaShanah — the Jewish New Year — for faith. The more we describe God's personal hand in redeeming us from Egypt, the more we instill faith in the hearts of our children. That is why even if the children know more than the parents do, it is a mitzvah for the parents to tell the story of the Exodus to their children, because the transmission of faith from parents to children on this night implants the love of God directly into the hearts of the children. This is the way we bridge the generation gap. We don't just tell the story to our children. We live the story, and we lodge faith within their souls.

Chapter Two

Batter Up: Self-Esteem and Believing in Your Divine Potential

In order to get a feel for running the "base paths" of this book, I would like you to see yourself as the batter in our baseball and Judaism model. Before you even pick up a bat you need to develop a mind-set of self-confidence that you can actually make contact with the ball as the pitcher hurls it your way. As you pick up the bat, which is a metaphor for facing the challenges of life, you must realize that you are capable of winning the game of life.

Baseball is a mind game. Success depends on your attitude. When you begin your day, you can get in the zone of success by becoming aware that the Commissioner of Baseball — God, the One who oversees the game — believes that you are good for the game. That is why you were sent onto the playing field — in other words, that's why you were sent down here into the world — to accomplish a mission that only you can achieve.

That's why you are playing. That's why you are in the world.

The commissioner is interested in promoting the "game of baseball," and he believes you can make a contribution to the game by playing for your team. He has delegated to your manager the day-to-day running of the team on and off the field. The manager obviously feels that you are good enough to play on the team, since he's placed you on the roster. God, too, feels you are good enough to play, since He's allowed you to wake up this morning. After all, some people did not get to play today. Unfortunately, they did not wake up this morning. You did. "Waking up" means becoming aware of the gift of life. You need not do anything. Just be in awe that you "are." This is an awareness of the art of "being."

When we open our eyes in the morning and become conscious of our renewed, reenergized selves, we as Jews say a short prayer: "*Modeh ani lefanecha* — I thank You, God, for returning my soul to me this morning." "*Rabbah emunasecha* — How great is *Your* faith."

Time out. Is this right? Shouldn't we be saying, "Thanks for returning my soul to me this morning and letting me step up to the plate again. How great is *my* faith in You, God"? But that is not what it says. The prayer says, How great is *Your* faith. Who does God have faith in? Is there someone that God believes in? The text actually says that the Commissioner (God) has faith...in *you*.

The spiritual source of this idea is that God has placed some of His own hitting power in you. God is the Source of your innate hitting and fielding power. That power is called your soul, or life force. The soul is a stream of breath from God, a piece of God's own batting energy placed within you.

That you are able to step up to the plate shows you have intrinsic value. This inner value is called your *tzelem Elokim*, your divine spark, or divine potential. It's the divine spark that God instilled in the first baseball player of all time, Adam. As it says in Genesis (2:7), "And God blew into Adam a living spirit." That divine image is the soul. Imagine having a baseball card of Adam. You do — and you *are* that card! And your baseball card — your self-image — is priceless.

In Jewish thought, every person in the world, regardless of religion, is born intrinsically pure and valuable. We are born with an innate goodness, otherwise known as Godliness. God is good, and He blew a spark of that goodness, that Godliness, into you when He gave you life. We remind ourselves of this every morning when we say in our morning prayers, "My God, the soul You placed within me is pure. You created it. You fashioned it. You breathed it into me. You safeguard it within me. And eventually You will take it from me and restore it to me in the time to come."

Getting up in the morning to pray is not, therefore, a religious act. It is a spiritual mantra to get us into a positive mindset to hit the pitches that are thrown to us each day. As he steps up to the plate, the batter — that's you — realizes that prayer is not for God. Prayer is for our own benefit. It allows *us* to survey the playing field and pick out a spot on the field toward which we want to hit the ball. God does not get anything from our prayers. He is perfect, and you can't improve on perfection. He is happy when we improve our batting stance and muster up the courage to take a swing. God is rooting for us from the Commissioner's Box.

Home Run Tips

- Since you are up to bat, that means you have the ability to get a hit. The very fact that it is your turn to bat means that you have the ability to make contact. Getting a hit means you can deal with life's curveballs — and you can get on base. The secret here is that you have the ability to meet life's challenges.

- If you gain this awareness that you are a capable individual, then you will have mastered the first tip for winning the game of life: You have to "show up" at the ballpark by being aware of the strengths and abilities that you bring to the team. You need to break out of the thinking that today is just another "at bat." You must realize that when you step up to the plate you can make it count. Which means that each moment that you are alive, every one of your actions counts and can make a difference on the baseball diamond called "life."

❧ The Commissioner of Baseball — God, who is responsible for the big picture, the game called life — believes that you are a starter. He believes that you can hit and that you can score a run for your team in particular and help advance the game of life in general. Faith means that God believes in you more than you believe in Him. With that inner confidence, you step into the batter's box.

❧ Value yourself. Become aware of your intrinsic Godly worth as you get up each day. You'll be sure to start the day with a winning attitude.

Chapter Three
Getting on Base: Believe in God Because He Believes in You

Some of the world's greatest philosophies have been created on the baseball field: "It's not if you win or lose, but how you play the game." This means that winning the game of life is not about amassing the most "toys," meaning assets and wealth. These things are temporal and don't bring lasting happiness. Ask the many rock stars and Hollywood actors, whose lives appear glitzy, successful, and filled with all the "good things" in life, whether the fast lane is worth it. Most will tell you it isn't. A fast-paced life without a stable family life, privacy, or consistent and meaningful values is not the stuff of real success. It may appear as if these American heroes are winning the game of life with fame and fortune, but even they will admit that their lives are mostly superficial and empty.

So how do you play the game to make your life count? Let us assume for a moment that the world has a purpose and a plan. Its existence is not an accident. If so, then as long as I relate to and work toward fulfilling the purpose of the universe, my life counts. So, having a relationship with the plan of the universe means that I am invited to have a relationship with the Planner of the universe. This is called "spirituality," having a relationship with the purpose and Planner of the universe.

We see this phenomenon in various aspects of life. Mankind as a whole is seeking a relationship with its own origins and so has sent up the Hubble telescope to photograph deep space and the moments of the origins of the stars and planets close to the big bang billions of years ago. Man is seeking a relationship with the Originator of the universe so he can figure out what he is doing here. When he finds out he has been adopted, an adopted child often tries to meet his birth parents. Why need he do that? His adoptive parents have nurtured and taken care of him. But he seeks his origins, and with that, perhaps insights into his "beginnings," and through that his pathway in life.

Now this concept of having a relationship with our Planner is a broad one. The Planner is pretty big and we are pretty small. So how do we relate to the Big Boss?

It makes sense that the Boss gave us some insights as to how to relate to Him, and we believe that He communicated the plan to us in the Torah. The 613 commandments in the Torah give us insight into how to relate to the Planner. They are 613 avenues of connection with Him. Commandments in Hebrew are called "mitzvos," which means "connectors." We connect with the Planner by activating the pathways of connection. These connections, or commandments, are the tools of the relationship.

Second, through our positive character traits, we exercise our spiritual essence to relate to the ultimate perfect Planner. If, however, I am lazy, angry, or mean, then these negative character traits will get in the way of my becoming close to the Planner, because I will not be the best I can be. And that is the purpose of life — to be the best I can be and thereby resemble the Planner, who is perfect. So life is all about self-transformation and self-perfection — as much as we can.

Let us now look at three areas of our lives where we can develop ourselves and become close to the perfection of the Planner: satisfying relationships, contributions to others, and growth through life's challenges:

Satisfying relationships: In the early 1960s, psychologist Harry Harlow performed a series of experiments where he placed newborn monkeys in a cage with a model of a "mother" monkey made of wire. The babies were fed by bottles attached to the wire frame. Without the tactile warmth and love of a real mother, the baby monkeys became psychotic — they lost touch with reality. A second group of monkeys was nurtured by a "mother" monkey comprised of a frame and fake fur, and they did a bit better than the first group. The only babies that were normal were those in a third group that was nurtured by their real mothers. This study pointed to the fact that people need love — which means they need a meaningful relationship — in order to be balanced and well-adjusted. Why?

The ultimate and closest human relationship is that of husband and wife who are living in a committed relationship with each other. The love and care that spouses show each other teaches them how to go beyond themselves and outside the box of their own ego.

When we do that, we learn how to relate to God. When we go beyond the "self" in the husband and wife relationship, the next step is to go beyond our own personal needs and self-interest and work toward partnering with the Planner of the universe. That is why *Song of Songs*, written by King Solomon, is a metaphor for the love between the Groom (God) and the bride (the Jewish people). Both marriage and a relationship with God require the sublimation of the ego and the development of humility. These lead to a deeper relationship with God, because there can only be one master of the universe — and that master is not me. So meaningful relationships between man and man help us relate to God.

Contributions to others: Man cannot live alone. Sure, he can survive, but he won't be fulfilled. Even though our natural instinct is for self-preservation and looking after our own ego, we cannot find emotional fulfillment by looking after ourselves alone. Human beings need to be givers. Why?

When we look for the goodliness and the Godliness in each other, then we are more likely to be good to each other. The purpose of being a giver and doing acts of kindness to others is to relate to the Godly spark within them. If we truly looked for the good in our spouse, children, and friends, then we would be relating to the Godlike part of them.

Doing good deeds helps us develop our character by making us more selfless, and that, in turn, helps us minimize our ego and make more room for God. We need to be givers and develop our giving natures so that we can resemble and relate better to God.

Growth through life's challenges: The purpose of life, according to Judaism, is to become the best person you can be. We are not here for physical satisfaction and pleasure. Life is a success when we gain wisdom through learning the lessons of life and growing through life's challenges. When we face life's ordeals and hit life's curveballs, we bring out more of our inner character. We become wiser, more caring, more sensitive, and more patient. We then develop our character and attain personal growth. Living life with integrity, sensitivity, and compassion is a winning formula. If you live by a system of consistent values, you actually win the game of life. Why?

Values like honesty, integrity, consistency, and kindness come from somewhere. They did not merely evolve as good ideas of social responsibility. They are good ideas because they are God ideas. God is the source of these values. When we develop these values, then we develop a closer relationship with the Source of these values — God Himself. We also become more Godlike.

Sometimes we need to be pushed to bring out these values in ourselves. Otherwise, we may remain complacent and self-centered. So at times God sends us tests which tend to stretch us. When we are sent challenges by God, our true and noblest character is revealed. Had it not been for the challenge, then our true character may have remained dormant. When our backs are against the wall and we are pushed, then more of our Godliness is revealed.

As the batter in our baseball model, take a moment to get to know your own batting strengths as you step up to the plate. Take an inventory of the talents and personal resources that you bring to the game. Look at the Baseball of Strengths chart below and fill in the six categories. This will help you define your character strengths and values. Once you do this, you will have greater self-awareness and self-confidence that you are a valuable player in this game. That will give you the initiative to get on base, where you will be in a position to score a run — to make a significant contribution to your family, community, and society.

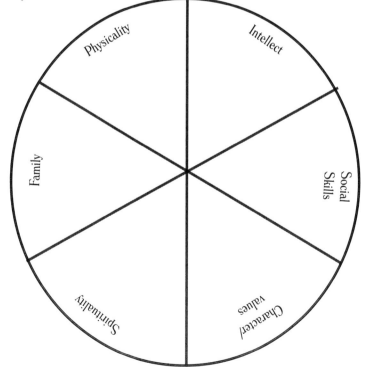

The six sections of the baseball represent six mini self–concepts — aspects of your personality — that make up your self-image. You relate to the world from the perspective of your intellect, social skills, character strengths, spiritual leanings, family background, and physical attributes.

Here's what you can do to get in the proper frame of mind to get up to bat. In each section of the baseball, write down two or three of your strengths or abilities. Here are some of the types of strengths you can include in each of the sections of your Baseball of Strengths.

Intellect: Are you street-smart? Do you have common sense? Are you book smart/academic? Are you quick-witted? Do you have a sense of humor? Are you a problem solver? Articulate? Intellectual? Organized?

Social skills: Are you a good friend? Do you have a close friend? Are you a good listener? Can you keep a confidence? Are you helpful to those in need? Are you involved in the community? Are you dependable and reliable? Do you encourage others? Are you committed? Loving? Generous? Tolerant? Understanding? Would you help a friend change a flat tire at three in the morning in the rain?

Character/Values: Which of these character traits best describe your strengths: affectionate, compassionate, considerate, appreciative, gracious, giving, patient, honest, sincere, creative, forgiving, calm, gutsy, disciplined, persistent, optimistic, resilient, spontaneous, visionary, ambitious, driven? (Add your own.)

Spirituality: Do you reflect on the meaning of life or on how to improve yourself? Do you believe in a higher power? Do you see God's hand in nature? Do you see a guiding hand in your life? Do you enjoy doing acts of kindness for others? What aspect of Judaism inspires you most?

Family: Does your family love and respect you? Do you have a voice in your family? Do you respect and love your spouse and children? Do you encourage your family? Does your family encourage you? Do you encourage independent thinking?

Physicality: Do you work out? Do you eat healthily? Do you help out around the house? Do you contribute to the upkeep of your workplace?

Now that you have surveyed your life strengths, you have probably noticed that these six sections are actually six pathways that you use to interact with the world. Your identity, or "self," is in essence your divine image or divine potential that God instilled in you when He created you. These divine character resources combine to reflect the "name" on the back of your uniform, which distinguishes you from the other players. There never has been nor will there ever be another person with your unique set of strengths. That's why you have been placed on the roster by your manager. He has matched your abilities and strengths with the needs of the team.

As you take an inventory of your strengths, you can begin to develop the attitude that you are a talented player in the game of life. If you see yourself as a person who can step up to the plate and get on base, you have the key ingredient to win the game — a positive self-image. By being in the game, you realize that God believes in you much more than you believe in Him.

Since September 11, 2001, almost every fire and police station in America has been adorned with a black and white sign that says "Believe." Why? The tragic events of 9/11 have shaken our national self-confidence. The terrorists have made us aware of our vulnerability. We have become paranoid and mistrustful. We have lost confidence in and stopped believing in ourselves. The Believe signs urge us to regain our self-confidence by once again *believing* in ourselves.

It used to be that baseball was simple, all-American fun. Since 9/11, what do we sing at almost every Major League game? "God Bless America." It even takes on spiritual significance. You can feel the mood in the stadium shift to spiritual mode as the flag waves in the wind and we all become silent, remove our hats, put our hands on our hearts, and ask for God's blessings.

A moment of soul has found its way into the midst of our national pastime.

But why at a ball game? Because when Americans get together at a ball game, the game takes on a spiritual quality. Here we are, thirty thousand people, celebrating our national sport, which represents striving for the American dream. Every ten-year-old boy in America dreams of becoming a hero and hitting the home run that will win the game for the home team. But there is something even more profound than that.

On 9/11 the terrorists attacked our national innocence. They attacked our way of life and our belief in ourselves. How do we get it back? The Commissioner has the answer: God, Bless America. Please, God, bless our way of life. You, God, gave us our lives, our freedom — and our way of life. You gave us our "selves" — our national and personal identity. When we call upon God to "bless America," we are asking Him to give us back our national pride and personal self-esteem. So baseball and faith have a lot in common. The common denominator is belief, belief in ourselves that we can live and enjoy our national pastime, and belief that we can get on base and play out our dreams.

Home Run Tips 𝄃

🔹 When we develop meaningful relationships, when we make a contribution to others, and when we develop our character and values through life's challenges, our lives gain deeper direction and meaning.

🔹 When you take an inventory of your "Baseball of Strengths" and become aware of your intellectual, social, character, spiritual, physical, and family strengths, you come to realize that you have a lot more talent and ability than you have ever given yourself credit for. These strengths are God-given, which means that God actually believes in you by giving you the abilities and resources to get on base and make a contribution to the game of life. It turns out that the concept of faith means that God believes in you more than you believe in Him. And that's okay. The more you realize that God is on your team, eventually you will develop a greater relationship with Him.

Chapter Four
Stepping Up to the Plate: Fear and Love of God

My sons Dovid and Yehudah play Little League Baseball in Baltimore for the Wellwood Baseball League, which is a wonderfully run organization where sportsmanship, good fun, and teamwork are the goals. Some kids get up to bat, but they only hope for a walk — the prospect of swinging the bat seems to frighten them. And the boy often does get his wish. He draws a walk, and the look on his face as he trots to first is one of sheer relief and joy. In his mind, a walk is his only way to get on base.

To watch this scenario being repeated a few times per inning is frustrating. Why? The purpose of playing Little League is to learn to get up there and give it your best shot. You don't want to just stand there and get called out on strikes. Or even get a walk. You want to put in some effort and take a swing, go after a pitch even if it is just outside the strike zone. This is one of the keys to success in life: Give it a shot. Don't let the walk happen. Don't let life just "happen." The goal is to *make* life happen. My telephone answering machine says: "Thanks for calling. Don't have a great day. Rather, make it a great day."

Classical Jewish philosophy posits that the human being is made up of three components: the body, the emotions, and the intellect. We spend most of our waking hours living on the level of our emotional selves. To name a few feelings we experience each day, we feel happy, angry, inspired, depressed, motivated, frustrated, annoyed, enthusiastic — and that is just before breakfast!

If we analyze the emotional self and break it down into its core, we find that there are only two fundamental emotions in life: love and fear. All other emotions stem from and are based on these two basic emotions. Love leads to positivity, encouragement, friendliness, contentment, enthusiasm, and joy. If you love yourself, and, even more important, if you *like* yourself, then you can like others and express these positive emotions to others and experience the richness of emotional contentment.

On the other end of the spectrum, fear leads to negativity, criticism, social withdrawal, meanness, restlessness, turmoil, sadness, and depression. If a person displays negativity or anger, for example, the foundation of the anger is fear. It is fear of inadequacy and reflects a lack of self-worth and self-esteem. For example, if someone is late for a meeting with me, and I show anger due to insult or hurt feelings, the underlying cause of this anger is fear that I am not sufficiently valued and appreciated.

In real life, we are sometimes afraid to "swing the bat." We lose our nerve to make that phone call, say what needs to be said, take a risk, enroll in that course, initiate that career move, or make that commitment. When we are afraid to move forward, it is coming from a place of fear within our psyche and soul. Deep down, we're afraid we aren't worthy or valuable enough. We're afraid we may fail.

Ultimately, the source of our fear comes from the way we look at our relationship with God. Our fear of God — that He has abandoned us or that He is out to get us — paralyzes us so much that we are afraid of venturing forward. Perhaps we might lose. We might make a mistake or hurt someone's feelings. We become defensive hitters who are just trying to protect the plate.

Some of us develop such a palpable fear of God that we fail to swing the bat because we are afraid of...success! If we get a hit, then we will be called upon to always get a hit. The pressure to always be "on" is too overwhelming for those who have not developed a healthy sense of self-confidence. The responsibility that comes with success is overwhelming, so we just stand there, frozen at the plate, and hope to go unnoticed and draw a walk.

The Hebrew word for fear is *yirah*. There are two types of *yirah*. One is fear that I will make a mistake and get zapped — so I act defensively. And there is a second type of *yirah* called *yiras haromemus*, awe of God and His world. If you see a waterfall, sunset, or mountain range and you stand there in awe, you are actually saying to yourself, *Wow, I can't do that! Whoever made that must be amazing!* I see God's hand in nature and am grateful that He decided to allow me to experience this particular inspiration. I can use this as an opportunity to develop my relationship with God by appreciating the sunset, the waterfall, and the lightning storm as God's personal gift to me. We are awestruck at the wondrous world we are privileged to live in. We want to explore, discover, and learn more about the world and our place in it.

When we apply the "awe" approach to hitting, then we want to be on base so badly that we become aggressive at the plate. We crave the excitement of being on base so much that we reach down for pitches and go after a pitch. The spiritual source of this attitude is one of positivity and love of life.

What is the secret of those people who have that joie de vivre? If you take their attitude to its source, you will find that what lies at its core is a love of God. We want to relate to our origin, our Source, and we reach out for a relationship with God.

In the classic Jewish work, *The Path of the Just*, Rabbi Moshe

Chaim Luzzatto states that the purpose of life is to "delight in God." How do we do that? When we are aware of and appreciate the benefits and kindnesses that God has given us — eyesight, hearing, taste, thinking, speech, creativity, the capacity to love and be loved — we enter into a mind-set of gratitude. I invite you to compose a list of twenty things for which you feel gratitude and keep that list with you. Review it daily. Use it to get yourself out of a bad mood. Use it to keep yourself in a good mood. Use it to create for yourself a mind-set of gratitude. Whenever I ask one of my friends how he is, he answers: "Grateful." And each time I hear that, I say to myself, *Why can't I have such a positive outlook on life? Wouldn't life look different if I did?*

All of these abilities come from somewhere. We did not create them ourselves. Feeling gratitude requires humility. It requires a quieting of the ego. This is no easy task. But when we develop an appreciation of life, the benefits are astounding. It translates into stepping up to the plate and swinging in energy and exuberance. We grab for life because we appreciate and yearn for the thrill and adventure of being part of God's "baseball diamond" — this wonderful opportunity we call "life."

In a prayer we say as we anticipate the coming of the Sabbath, we symbolically go out into the fields on the outskirts of the city to welcome the Sabbath Queen and sing: "*Nafshi cholas ahavasecha* — My soul yearns for Your love." I want to be a base runner because I love the game, and I want to hustle down the base paths and enjoy the excitement of competing on God's playing field. In this way each new game — each new day — becomes an adventure of playing the game of life.

It is the coach's job to teach the player not to fear the ball, and not to fear even getting hit by the ball. This means you need to learn to take a stand for what you believe in. Taking an assertive stance at the plate means that you feel you have a right to your opinion and you are going to take a stand for yourself.

Of course, the coach should also teach the player how to

avoid getting hit. He should teach him how to keep his eye on the ball — to concentrate on the task at hand. And he should teach him how to strike out with grace and sportsmanship.

The coach should also teach him that when he strikes out — and he will strike out — he shouldn't throw his bat. This is as important a lesson as actually getting on base. We are all going to strike out sometimes in life, and we need to learn how to handle that disappointment and focus on the next inning. Even the best hitters strike out or fail to get a hit 70 percent of the time. And here is another one of life's secrets: every time we strike out, it builds our humility — and character.

Home Run Tips 🏏

🔹 When we face a challenge in life, we don't have to become depressed when things don't go our way. We can realize that God is teaching us something about life through this challenge and that we can improve and grow through the experience. This is what we mean when we say that God is "with us" in our pain.

🔹 There are only two key foundation emotions in life: love and fear. If someone if angry with you, it is probably due to an underlying fear that you don't value him. Anger comes from fearing that you are not good enough. If you work on yourself and start valuing yourself, you can learn to transform your fear of a lack of intrinsic value into a love of self where you are aware of and appreciate your strengths and abilities. Then you can develop a positive "I can" attitude and become assertive at the plate and in life.

Chapter Five
Getting a Hit: Reaching Your Life's Destiny

B efore we try to get a hit, let's review the goals of baseball and the object of the game. We need to do this at the beginning of any endeavor to know where to direct our efforts. If not, we will become victims of the winds of chance, as the great baseball philosopher, Yogi Berra, once said: "If you don't know where you are going, you'll probably end up somewhere else."

The goal in baseball is to score more runs than the other team does and thereby win the game. You score runs by stepping up to the plate, swinging the bat, and hitting the ball so that it isn't caught. When the ball lands on the field in fair territory, you can run to first base, then to second, then to third, and, if you make it back to home plate, you score a run. Getting on first is better than striking out. Getting a double is better than getting a single. A triple is better than a double, and a home run is the best of all. It is better to be at second base than at first base because the runner is closer to the goal; he is in a better position to score a run — and scoring helps you win the game.

What we have discovered here is the secret philosophy of

baseball. Baseball is a game of relative values. Singles, doubles, triples, and home runs are relative to each other in value. We also have discovered that scoring a run is the yardstick by which we measure the relative value of each hit. If you get a hit, then we can determine how valuable that hit is by whether the hit caused a player to score a run. So besides having a relative value system, baseball also has an ultimate value system — scoring runs — through which all other values derive their meaning.

The ultimate focus of baseball is scoring the most runs and winning the game. All of the players' efforts are directed toward this one goal. Now let's relate the ultimate meaning of baseball to life. How do you win the game of life? Is it the person with the most toys, the biggest house, and the most vacations who wins the game? Our society seems to think so. The heroes of America are the athletes, the movie stars, and the rich and famous.

Let's take a deeper look at real values. The reason we need money and a livelihood is to finance a life of purpose and meaning. We do not live to work; we work to live. Making money and having the newest electronic gadgets is not called winning. These gadgets may bring us temporary and fleeting pleasure, but pleasure is not the same thing as happiness. Pleasure is the excitement or soothing of our five senses. These are merely physical pleasures.

John Kluge is someone who found ultimate meaning. A fabulously wealthy man, he heads a network of major companies. He has "been there, done that, and has bought almost all the T-shirts" that money can buy. When asked what was the most meaningful thing he had ever accomplished, he related the following story. A boy in England needed a lifesaving operation, and there was only one doctor in America who could perform it. So John Kluge paid for the family to fly to America and covered the cost of the operation. "This," said Kluge, "was the most meaningful thing I ever did."

Kluge used his wealth to change someone's life for the better.

Not only that — he saved a life. He also transformed himself. He grew in character. He not only gave charity, but he transformed himself into a charitable person. That is the purpose of life: to make this world a better place than when we entered it, and that should be the ultimate focus of our actions.

The Olympic Games — the legacy of the ancient Greeks — emphasizes athletic prowess. The problem is that the competition is standardized. All the athletes have to hit the same target, make the same basket, cross the same finish line. Only those who are tall and strong are in the race. All others are out of the competition. In Judaism, everyone has his own finish line. You are not competing against others; you compete only against yourself. The goal is to achieve your personal best. Being the world's best is not important. Becoming the world's best "me" is.

A father once brought his child who had Down syndrome to receive a blessing from a great Torah sage. The rabbi stood up as they came into the room. The rabbi's students asked the rabbi why he was standing up for this man, who was not a particularly great Torah scholar. "I am not standing up for the father," said the sage. "I am standing up for the child. If the child came into this world with limited potential for growth, it means he has a near-perfect *neshamah* (soul) and does not need to grow that much in this world. I am standing up in awe of a near-perfect *neshamah*."

The rabbi was pointing out to us that it is not how much you accomplish but how much you have grown that counts. In this case, growth can occur over millennia, through various reincarnations, until a person achieves his or her ultimate destiny. Judaism does actually believe that people can come back into this world after they die in another reincarnation called a *gilgul*. The goal is to perfect the soul the first time you are in this world. But if you don't, you are sent back into the world to continue the journey toward self-perfection.

The goal in this world is to strive to achieve as much character growth as we can. Let us look at the game of baseball in this context and see how we can become the best players we can in the game of life.

The first motivation for living is "to find happiness," which we associate with physical pleasure. This can be considered hitting a single. You get on base when you enjoy the creature comforts of life. Many people live for these pleasures and believe that when they have experienced these pleasures they have "made it" in life. In fact, happiness through physical pleasure is the first, most superficial motivation for living.

There is a higher motivation for living: loving another person. Many people would be willing to give up all the physical pleasures of life for the pleasure of loving another. Loving someone is considered hitting a double — getting to second base. It makes all the pain go away. You can conquer most physical obstacles if you are motivated by love. Love is closer to the ultimate value — which is spirituality and meaning. The reason is that love creates an environment of acceptance. And acceptance by someone you care about deeply can set the stage for self-acceptance. Love gets you closer to knowing yourself.

How do you get a triple? What is a higher spiritual value than love? If your spouse said to you, "If you really loved me, you would rob a bank for me," or, "If you really loved me, you would kill for me," would you? Of course not. There are certain things you would not do for love, because living with values and integrity is an even higher motivation for living than love is.

Every soldier who has gone to war has given up love in exchange for his values and integrity. As Nathan Hale, the great American patriot, said before he was executed by the British in 1776, "I only regret that I have but one life to give for my country." When you give up love in the name of integrity, you have hit a triple.

This motivation for living is even more intangible than love. It is a philosophy, a way of living with conscience, of being able to live with yourself. This is even closer to the ultimate value of spirituality and meaning than physical pleasure and love are.

Even if you score runs, you still need to win the game. You can win the game by living a life of spirituality and conducting yourself according to the highest standards of behavior and morality. Living this way enables us to have a relationship with the One who set up the system, the Commissioner of Baseball, God. He made us, and He wants to give us all an opportunity to taste the best thing life has to offer — God Himself. So He gives each of us the opportunity to achieve our respective purposes in life by having a relationship with Him through living by His standards.*

How do you get a home run? If you make a positive contribution to society and leave a lasting legacy in the world — that's a homer. Making your life count is even more intangible than living with integrity. It can consist of an idea or project that improves others' quality of life. Because it is closer to the ultimate value, making a contribution to society is a higher motivation for living than enjoying physical pleasure and being in love are. It's coming full circle and scoring a home run. You have made your life journey and have come "home" with a life-enhancing run — a benefit for humanity.

Now let's analyze each of the relative values in depth: physical pleasure, love, integrity, and creating a legacy.

Home Run Tips 𝄡

٭ The ultimate value in life is to live a spiritual life, which means a meaningful and purposeful life, making a positive contribution to your family, friends, community, and society. I did not merely live and die. Rather, I lived a life in which I made a contribution to others. The by-product of living this kind of life is true happiness. Victor Frankl terms this motivation for living "a search

---

* This is based on the classic work of Jewish philosophy, *Derech Hashem* (*The Way of God*), by Rabbi Moshe Chaim Luzzatto.

for a meaningful life." When man finds meaning, he finds himself. And he wins the game.

◈ Judaism is not a religion. It is a spiritual system designed to help all people achieve the ultimate meaning in life, which is developing yourself into the best person you can become. Judaism provides a framework for "becoming." We cannot sit back and say, "I have my faults —that's the way I am and I am not changing." Living a Jewish life is a process of self-transformation.

Chapter Six

Hitting a Single: Physical Pleasure

I magine that I am a roving reporter and I am interviewing people about the purpose of life. It's likely that a large proportion of people would answer that the purpose of life is to be happy. Happiness is a good thing. So let's analyze what we mean by happiness. Here is our working model for those activities and endeavors that make us happy:

FOOD	ACTIVITIES
Tacos	Exercise
Steak	Massage
Wine	Whirlpool
Cheese Cake	Sunbathing
Barbecue	Sleep

I am sure you can add your own happiness triggers in both of these categories. We live in a society that is absolutely brimming with opportunities for physical pleasures. In any American city with a population of over one million, there are thousands of restaurants. That means your average American diner could go out to a restaurant every day for the next few years and never eat at the same restaurant twice! Now that is bound to make a lot of people happy, isn't it?

Well, consider this. Let me describe an eating experience that I am sure you have gone through at least once. You were a bit stressed, and to help yourself relax, you reached for a pint of ice cream, a bag of potato chips, or a box of cookies. You took one spoonful of ice cream, one potato chip, or one cookie, and it tasted good and brought a bit of a smile to your face. Then you reached for another, and it also made you feel good. And then you reached for another. Well, somewhere between cookie number three and the last cookie in the box (or the last chip in the bag or the last lick of ice cream all the way at the bottom of the container) you went into autopilot. You barely tasted what you were eating, you were only half-conscious of what you were doing, and you ended up with a stomachache. What had started as a pleasant enough exercise in relaxation left you feeling ill, bloated, and embarrassed that you were now licking the inside of the lid of an ice cream container. How is it that a simple food experience that usually produces happiness ended with your feeling worse at the end than when you started?

We have just described the problem with the pursuit of physical pleasures as a means to achieving happiness. On the one hand, we seem to have a natural interest in and ever-present desire for a wide variety of pleasures. This appetite of ours begins at an early age and gets more voracious the older we become. Where once pureed carrots and applesauce were enough to make us gurgle gleefully, it now takes two scoops of chocolate hazelnut supreme ice cream and a latte topped with a bit of whipped cream and a pinch of cinnamon to get us excited. And even then, before long we are searching for a newer, more exciting ice cream flavor and a more extravagant latte-cappuccino combo.

There are at least three problems with physical pleasures:

1. You get desensitized to them. The very thing that started off giving you so much pleasure goes flat over time and loses its zing at best, and makes you sick — sometimes literally — at worst. After a while, you can't even look at it anymore.

2. Once it's over, it's over. After you've finished the last lick of your ice cream cone, how long does that sensation of pleasure last? A minute? An hour? A week? Unfortunately, physical pleasures tend to be fleeting.

3. You can't build on them. Our experience of Chinese food doesn't get deeper and more satisfying as time goes by. It's not as if each experience builds upon the previous one, so that the thirtieth time you order chicken lo mein it's a far greater culinary delight because you had it twenty-nine times before that. Each time you go out for Chinese food, you are basically starting from scratch.

If you contrast physical pleasure with another kind of pleasure in life, like the pleasure of friendship, it's even clearer why physical pleasures do not meet their high billing:

1. You never tire of friendship. True friendship isn't something you get sick of. Three hours with a good friend whets your appetite for more friendship. Three pints of ice cream leaves you never wanting to see ice cream again — at least not for a week.

2. You can build on friendship. When friends spend a day together, that shared experience becomes the basis for future experiences. The next time they spend a day together, that new experience doesn't exist in a vacuum. Each experience is another brick in the building of their relationship. You cannot build on your relationship with the steak you just devoured, no matter how delicious it was.

3. You can build on the pleasure of friendship. With physical pleasure, once it's over, it's gone. In contrast, the pleasure of time spent with a friend lingers. This residual pleasure can stay with you for days, months, and even years to come. When old friends meet again, their past is still very much a part of them. They can pick up where they left off.

We seem to be hardwired for pursuing happiness through physical pleasures, but these pleasures end up to be fleeting and inevitably leave us feeling frustrated, unsatisfied, and sometimes even sick. We are stuck on the treadmill of pursuing ever more exotic physical pleasures that end up disappointing us. The "pleasure principle" fails to bring us real, lasting happiness.

Historically, there have been two primary approaches to this dilemma:

1. *The Roman approach*, which can be summarized as "Eat and drink, for tomorrow we die" (Isaiah 22:13). This is the approach of wild indulgence, which says, "Even though physical pleasures may not be perfect, why fight your basic nature? Just indulge until you get sick and tired of your indulgences and then, well, start all over again."

2. *The ascetic approach*, which is common to many Eastern religions and spiritual disciplines and which finds its fullest expression in the world of the monastery and the life of monks, priests, and nuns. The ascetic seeks to deny the body's indulgences through fasting for extended periods of time, exposing oneself to harsh and painful elements for extended periods of time, and being celibate. The goal of these practices is to break the body of its desires and appetites and to convince it that it can subsist on very little, even in a state of extreme discomfort. This has the intended dual effect of neutralizing the body and liberating the soul.

The Jewish approach to physical pleasure is unlike either of the other two. The Jerusalem Talmud sums up this approach with the following statement: "Rabbi Yosi says: Man will have to give an accounting to God for every fruit that was presented to him and which he denied himself." This means that we are allowed, and, in fact, encouraged to enjoy the pleasures of life, and we are expected to elevate these pleasures to a higher plane by connecting the pleasure with its divine Source.

This idea finds practical expression every week on Shabbos, which begins at sundown on Friday and ends at nightfall on Saturday. First, there is an obligation to eat three festive meals every Shabbos. And the law is that one's finest foods should be served on one's finest dishes at the Shabbos meals. Second, Shabbos (as well as all Jewish holidays) begins with Kiddush, a special blessing sanctifying the day that is recited over a glass of wine. Again, it is most appropriate to use a fine wine that one particularly enjoys when reciting Kiddush.

The Jewish attitude to physical pleasure is rooted in the Jewish understanding of the essential spiritual nature of the human being. Judaism views the human being not as a body, and not as a soul, but as a fusion of the physical and the spiritual. In essence, the body and the soul are partners, not adversaries.

Let's take a deeper look at Shabbos, whose observance is the fourth of the Ten Commandments.

On Friday night we come to the Shabbos dinner dressed in our finest clothes and sit down to a beautifully set table brimming with an assortment of delicious foods. Sounds a bit like Roman indulgence, doesn't it? There is a big difference, however. You see, in Rome they donned their finest tunics and sat down to a feast for one reason only, and that was to achieve the greatest amount of physical pleasure possible. The pleasure was an end in and of itself. The Shabbos dinner is just the opposite. The purpose of a delicious and beautifully presented meal is to elevate and energize the body so that it feels good about life, so to speak, and happily joins with the soul in the pursuit of spirituality, which is the deeper meaning of Shabbos. The pleasure of the meal is a means, not an end. It is the means to take physicality and dedicate it to a higher purpose: connecting with the Source of physical pleasure — God.

The Shabbos meal begins with the pouring of a full cup of wine, reciting a blessing, and then making sure everyone enjoys the wine with his meal. And get this: If a second, superior wine is brought to the table after Kiddush, another blessing is made specifically in recognition of the arrival of the better wine. Sounds a bit bacchanalian, doesn't it? Once again, there's a difference, and this time it's twofold.

The first difference, again, is the ends-versus-means difference. Wine provides a special kind of lift. It has the ability to relax us, loosen our inhibitions, and lift our spirits. All of these are positive feelings that enable the body to sense the deeper pleasure of joining with the soul in the higher quest for spirituality. It expands the sense of physical consciousness in order to make room for the greater, spiritual, soul consciousness of Shabbos. As we expand our spiritual consciousness from the mundane activities of the week into the holiness and spirituality of the Sabbath, we take a taste of wine. The taste is merely an expansion of physical consciousness to match the expansion of spiritual consciousness from the mundane of the workaday week to the holiness of the Shabbos. Drinking for the sake of drinking is ultimately debasing. On the other hand, drinking for a meaningful purpose transforms a high that inevitably drags one down into a high that can lift one to the heights.

In fact, that is why we drink wine at major life-cycle milestones. At a wedding ceremony, when the consciousness of self, of one's identity, expands from one person to a couple, we make a blessing over wine. One moves from self-absorption to "other" consciousness. The physical expansiveness that a taste of wine ever so slightly provides is necessary to contain and reflect the expansion of selfhood from singlehood to marriage.

At a circumcision ceremony, we also make a blessing over wine and take a small taste. The circumcision marks the expansion of the family by adding a new member to the community and the covenant of the Jewish people. The wine symbolically expands our minds beyond the purely rational, and this reflects the expansion of the parents' spiritual consciousness to a consciousness beyond themselves — in the creation of the next generation.

Another difference between the Jewish and Roman approaches to physical pleasure is reflected in the blessings we recite before drinking wine. The Shabbos Kiddush blessings focus our attention on God, the spiritual potential of life, and the meaning of being Jewish. At the very moment that a good glass of wine is about to provide us with a lift, the blessings raise our sights and focus us on where we want to go with that lift.

We want to channel all of our physical tendencies toward the spiritual goal of serving God on Shabbos. This is called a spiritual "rest," or connection to God, and it gives meaning, direction, and context to our physical pursuits on the six days of the workweek.

The most fundamental tenet of Judaism is contained in the words of the Shema, which a Jew is required to say in prayer twice a day: "Hear O' Israel, the Lord our God, the Lord is One" (Deuteronomy 6:4). This is not just a declaration that there is one God and not two or more, but a statement about God's essential Oneness, His ultimate and complete unity. The union of a husband and a wife, the fusion of two into one, is a window, so to speak, on the ultimate unity of God. According to the Talmud, *Song of Songs* is the holiest book in all the prophetic writings in the Bible. On the surface it is about the love between a man and a woman, and beneath the surface it is a metaphor for the ultimate spiritual experience, the experience of unity between God and the Jewish nation.

Let's go back and focus for a moment on the statement in the Talmud about enjoying all fruits with which we are presented. A basic question has to be asked here: Why does God care if I pass up the chance to taste a kumquat or not? Is it really such a big deal?

In truth, this concept reveals a fundamental perspective on Jewish spirituality and on the deepest meaning of our existence.

It won't come as a surprise to you that Judaism understands God to be the ultimate Source of all existence. Part of our understanding of God is that He lacks nothing, and since He lacks nothing, He has no needs. This being the case, He didn't create the universe, the kumquat, and everything in between because He needs any of it. Creation isn't for God; it's for us. All of creation, in the Jewish way of relating to it, is a gift — a gift that we are meant to enjoy and benefit from, a gift that expresses, like all gifts do, the desire for a relationship. The issue is: How do we relate to the gifts that are the expression of God's relationship with us?

In general, there are three ways the recipient of a gift can respond:

1. You can accept the gift with an attitude of "it's coming to me" and take the gift for granted. This is a self-centered attitude, and we all know what it's like to try to have a relationship with someone who is self-centered.

2. You can reject the gift. Think about the last time someone rejected one of your gifts. That didn't do much for the relationship, did it?

3. You can graciously accept the gift and enjoy it. The warm acceptance of a gift fosters a sense of closeness and deepens the relationship. This is how it is with God. When we accept and enjoy the gifts with which He has filled our world, we foster our relationship with Him. We recognize and acknowledge that He cares about us enough to supply us with this world full of fruit baskets. It is our way of saying, "Thanks for caring, thanks for having me in mind, thanks for relating." And when you think about it, what deeper spirituality could there be than having a sense of connection and relationship with the Source of all existence?

All the ideas about the spiritual dimension of life's physical pleasures are contained in the concept of what are called in Hebrew *"birchos hanehenin,"* blessings over that which gives us pleasure. In Jewish life there are special blessings we say before and after we eat food and blessings we recite when we smell fragrant spices or flowers. In fact, with many things we enjoy from God's world, we are obliged to connect with Him by making a blessing, which acknowledges Him as the Source of this gift.

The notion of saying a blessing before eating food does four things:

1. *Blessings enable us to eat with a sense of mindful consciousness.* Being aware that what we are about to enjoy is a gift, and enjoying that gift in the context of a relationship with God puts us in touch with our sense of gratitude.

2. *Blessings provide an extra degree of focus on detail.* We make different types of blessings over vegetables, fruit, and manufactured items. Having the chance to make various types of blessings, as opposed to one catch-all blessing, allows us to see the rich variation of pleasures that God has provided for us, each with a different taste, texture, fragrance, and color that work together to create unique packages of pleasure.

3. *Blessings lift our sights.* They focus us on God; on a deeper purpose in life; on things of Jewish value, like the land of Israel and Jerusalem. Blessings guide our consciousness so that we stay focused on keeping physical pleasure in its proper context, as a means to greater ends.

4. *Blessings help you enjoy your ice cream.* They are a powerful line of defense against the autopilot experience that ends in a guilt-ridden stomachache, and they help you maintain a sense of presence that allows you to actually savor the good tastes in life.

Now let's look back at our baseball diamond and our runner on first base. With our understanding of the Jewish view toward physical pleasure, we have just hit a single, which is good.

But there is still a way to go until we score a run and win the game. In the next chapter we will discuss getting to second base with a good, solid double.

Home Run Tips 人

- The body and soul are partners. The Jewish approach to physical pleasure is neither one of indulgence, because that would be placing undue emphasis on one of the "partners," nor the way of the ascetic, because that would demean one of the "partners." The Jewish approach is to see the body as a full partner with the soul in the attainment of a spiritual life. If you want to know who you really are, you need to get in touch with that aspect of yourself where your body and soul meet.

Chapter Seven
A Stand-Up Double: Love

At this point in our game of baseball the announcer would say, "What a hit! He's around first base, and heading for second with a solid stand-up double." Remember, every hitter would rather hit a double than a single, and when it comes to physical pleasure and love, all the delicious physical pleasures in the world don't even compare to the pleasure of loving another person.

If one person loves another with the intensity of a 10 out of 10 and the other party loves with the intensity of a 5 out of 10, then the overall closeness of the relationship will be...5. Love is only as strong as its weakest link. The person who loves with the intensity of 10 can't force the person who loves with the intensity of 5 to love more intensely. On the other hand, we are not interested in weak or superficial relationships, since they are unfulfilling. We are looking for depth, closeness, and a mutual intensity of 10. How do we get that satisfying, deep kind of love?

I would like to suggest an answer based on a theory of the famous psychologist Herman Adler, who has posited the theory of "unfinished business." Each of us has unfinished business, unresolved issues from our childhood. If one spouse understands the unfinished business of the other spouse, then each can help the other complete his. Here are some examples:

1. *A child who was heavily disciplined or abused* as a child emerges from childhood with the unfinished business of needing validation, a sense of security, and protection. Let us say this child grows up and gets married. Call this person Spouse 1. If his spouse, Spouse 2, understands this and helps Spouse 1 resolve or complete his unfinished business, then Spouse 1 will feel that Spouse 2 has fulfilled her needs. This sense of fulfillment is what we call "love."

2. *A child who was outshone by an older sibling* who was a star student, athlete, or "perfect kid" will emerge from childhood with the unfinished business of needing praise, a healthy dose of self-esteem, and respect for who she is. When this child (call this person Spouse 1) gets married, he or she will need his spouse (Spouse 2) to understand this unfinished business. If Spouse 2 understands the situation, empathizes, and provides what Spouse 1 needs, then Spouse 1 will feel that Spouse 2 is there for him, and the resulting feeling will be love toward Spouse 2.

3. *A child who was the youngest in the family and grew up in a family of large and powerful personalities* might have the unfinished business of needing to assert herself, and she may have a streak of aggressiveness. While growing up, she needed to make herself heard — hence, her assertive behavior. When this assertive child gets married (call her Spouse 1) then Spouse 2 needs to become aware of Spouse 1's upbringing and unfinished business. Spouse 2 can help Spouse 1 complete her unfinished business by influencing her to temper her assertiveness. He can help her realize that aggressiveness was an "old" need that has become unnecessary because of a new set of circumstances. Spouse 1 will then be more content and will love Spouse 2 for helping her grow and resolve her unfinished business.

In helping one's spouse resolve his unfinished business, each spouse becomes a giver by trying to understand the unresolved issues of his partner and then helping his spouse complete his character growth.

Let us contrast this type of love, where one spouse really reaches out to help the other, with the "feel-good factor" of love. Let me illustrate with an example. Think of a food that you really, *really* love. For me it would be steak. Now, if I am really honest with myself, I would ask myself the following: "How do I show my love for this steak? I take Bessie the Cow, and I slaughter her, tan and hide her, chop her up, and broil her until she is well done. Then I eat the steak that Bessie has so kindly provided, with barbecue sauce. Is this how I treat something that I truly love? If I *really* loved steak, I would take Bessie into my backyard and groom her, spend time with her, and talk to her like I talk to my plants! What I need to realize is that I don't actually love my steak; what I really love is...myself. I don't love that steak for any reason other than what it does for me, which is that it tastes good and makes *me* feel good.

If I could summarize the Jewish perspective on relationships, I would say the following: Life is about relationships. And we can find this underlying theme of relationships encoded in the inner fabric of the Ten Commandments, which are always depicted as two sets of five commandments on two tablets of stone, like this:

1. *I am God* — Believe in Me	6. *Don't murder*
2. *Have no other gods* — Including money	7. *Don't commit adultery*
3. *Don't take God's Name in vain*	8. *Don't steal*
4. *Observe the Sabbath*	9. *Don't give false testimony*
5. *Honor your parents*	10. *Don't be jealous*

According to Jewish tradition, the reason the Ten Commandments are divided into two sets of five is to illustrate two types of relationships. The five commandments on the left side all have to do with one's relationship with God, while the five on the right side all have to do with one's relationship with other people. What these commandments are all about is relationships.

Additionally, we have a tradition from our Sages that the Ten Commandments are actually supracommandments, and that all 613 commandments in the Torah are subsets of these ten. For instance, our Sages say that if you don't pay a worker his wages on time, it's like stealing from him. If you embarrass or gossip about someone, the resulting embarrassment is a form of murder. When looked at this way, all of the commandments in the Torah can be listed under the one general heading of relationships of decency and respect toward others.

This explains a famous statement by the great Talmudic sage Rabbi Akiva, who lived in the second century CE: When the Torah says, "Love your neighbor as yourself," this is the singular, all-encompassing principle of the Torah. All the rest is commentary on this one underlying theme (Talmud Tractate *Shabbos* 31a).

It's no wonder that we all sense that a life devoid of deep, meaningful relationships is a crippled life. Just like we are hardwired with appetites for physical pleasures, we are similarly hardwired with a drive and need for relationships.

But here, too, there is a problem. The problem with physical pleasures is that they seem to be fleeting and desensitizing. The problem with relationships is that they seem to be inherently messy. Once again, we are faced with a dilemma: On the one hand, we all need and yearn for rich, deep relationships. At the same time, we know that the deeper relationships get, the more prone they are to being painful, stress inducing, heartbreaking, and messy.

What's a person to do? Where can we find a model for healthy relationships?

The answer lies in the parent-child relationship. We have all at one time or another been a child or a parent. There is no escaping it. One way or another, we all have experience with the parent-child relationship.

I believe that the relationship of a parent to a child affords us the most pristine look at the essential elements of *all* deep relationships. Of course, the parent-child relationship can also be complicated and disheartening. At the same time, it is so naturally deep and durable that it offers the best opportunity to see beyond the mess to the ultimate potential of all deep relationships.

Let us analyze four aspects of the parent-child relationship, and then apply these principles to the other key relationship: marriage. Then we will have the bedrock principles necessary for a deep, loving, and long-lasting marriage, as well as insight into the heart and soul of being a parent, either now or in the future. And once you've got those relationships down, the rest are a breeze.

Principle 1: Faults. Question: Who loves you more than anyone in the world? Your mother, or your spouse? Now here is the question: Is your mother/father/husband/wife aware that you have any faults or shortcomings? Of course they are, and most likely they are keenly aware of your shortcomings. The question then is, if they are so aware of your shortcomings, why do they love you so much?

We just debunked the myth that says "love is blind." Love isn't blind at all. Love actually sharpens our eyesight. The more you love someone, the *more* of them you see and become aware of.

Love is a function of perception, a particularly focused perception. Love is a function of seeing beauty, goodness, and virtue in another human being. The more beauty and goodness we see, the more we love, and the more we love, the more beauty we see. At the same time, the more we see of a person, the more likely we are to become keenly aware of his shortcomings.

However, it's the awareness of all the beauty that enables us to stay focused on the good, and to overlook and minimize the negative. We look at the package, at the big picture.

Here is an example. The following are the words of Bill McVeigh, father of Timothy McVeigh, the Oklahoma City bomber, who was convicted of murdering over 150 people in the bombing of a federal building in Oklahoma City (quoted in the *New York Times*, April 8, 2001):

> I wish people were interested in the Timothy McVeigh who, to me, is more than the Oklahoma City bomber. I would like to tell them about the kid at home, the kid who worked at Burger King, the kid on the bicycle. I try to think of him as a kid. I call him "Timmy." Tim is the one who did this bad thing. Timmy is the kid I remember. I love him. No doubt about it. I don't love what he did.

When most people think of Timothy McVeigh, they envision a cold, calculating, murderous monster who killed many and shattered the lives of many more. When Bill McVeigh thinks of him, he thinks about Timmy, the kid on the bicycle.

When it comes to Timothy McVeigh, it's we who are blind. We are blinded because all we see is the evil. His father, on the other hand, sees the entire person. He sees the beauty, despite the hideous act.

So principle number one is this: Love is a powerful and pleasurable feeling that is rooted in seeing beauty and virtue in another human being. Where there is love, there is a perception of beauty, and for love to endure, there must always be a perception of beauty. When we see beauty, we focus on the whole beautiful package of the person — and put his faults in the perspective of his overall goodness.

Principle 2: Commitment. Commitment is the willingness to forgo personal pleasure and benefit for the sake of someone or something else. In relationships, commitment is the willingness to make sacrifices for someone other than yourself. In his parents, a child sees and learns just how deep one's commitments can be. There is very little that parents won't do for their children. Parents are deeply committed people, and all deep relationships require deep commitment.

Principle 3: Giving. I want you to picture someone in your mind's eye who you consider to be a beautiful human being, a truly beautiful person. Now I am going to predict for you the person you chose. The central quality inherent in the person you pictured was the quality of giving, of being an outwardly focused, caring, and "other-oriented" person. You probably pictured someone like Mother Teresa. Isn't it fascinating how all of us, without any prior discussion, naturally have the same concept of what makes for a beautiful human being? It's being a giver. Giving is beautiful; taking isn't.

Now let's think about the relationship of a parent to a child. To be a parent means to be a giver. Children need and take, while parents give. Parenting is an incredible training ground for being a giver. If parents learn nothing else, they learn how to give. But there is more — parents also learn that it's a pleasure to give. Children do enjoy taking and receiving, but not nearly as much as parents enjoy giving. That is why parents love their kids more intensely than kids love their parents. It is because the parents are giving much more than the kids are. The more we give to a person, the more we love him. One of the opportunities of parenthood is to develop the quality that makes ordinary people into beautiful human beings: the quality of giving.

The Hebrew word for "love," which is spelled *ahavah*, contains within it the word *hav*, which means "to give." In Hebrew, the definition of a word is its function. That is why it is called the holy tongue. And that is why scholars want to study Hebrew in the original. In Hebrew the definition of love is to give. So we see that giving is a key to love, and a key to all deep relationships.

Principle 4: Soul. We are all awestruck by a newborn baby. Adults seem to melt when they see one. In a newborn we intuit the presence of something transcendent. That something is the soul. It is the life force in its purest from. A tiny, helpless baby causes us to focus on the deepest part of ourselves, namely, our souls — our own life force.

Our vision is often blurred by so much exterior and surface baggage that it's hard to see the soul. We get caught up in superficialities. With children, it's easy. You look at a child, and you see a soul.

So the fourth key to deep relationships is the ability to see not just the beauty, but the deepest source of that beauty, the essence of every human being: the soul.

The soul is the life force because it is the breath of God. The soul is known in Hebrew as a *chelek Elokai mima'al,* a piece of God from above. That is why the soul lives forever. When a person dies, his or her essence — the eternal part of the person — becomes reunited with its Source, God.

Now that we have culled some insights into relationships from the parent-child relationship, let us apply these principles to marriage.

Principle 1: Faults. There is a problem with love in the context of marriage that plagues single people, and even for married couples it can be a source of uneasiness and distress. We all want to be in love with the person we are married to, and at the same time some people have had the experience of being in love and then losing interest. The question that nags at us is, how do I know that my feelings for the person I marry will remain strong?

Remember that we exploded the myth that "love is blind"? Well, the truth is, there is something that *is* blind. It's called romance. Here people are focused on the more superficial aspects of their relationship. They are concerned more with chemistry than with inner beauty, which we have defined as real giving. Their delight is more in the fleeting experiences of fun than in the routine of day-to-day living and giving. In fact, though their feelings may run as deep as the seas, people involved in these kinds of relationships are standing on a sandy reef that is just waiting to be washed away. And so we have a 50 percent divorce rate. Chemistry does not translate into the long-term key to successful relationships — constant giving.

The crux of the problem is this: When people think they have fallen in love, they haven't. They have fallen into romance. Their disastrous mistake is confusing romance with love. Romance comes and goes — that is its nature. Love, because it is focused on the deeper, enduring aspects of a person, our giving nature, is enduring — that is *its* nature. If you want relationships to succeed, focus on giving and self-sacrifice.

Principle 2: Commitment. There is a rumor floating around that a lot of people these days are having a hard time making commitments. It's called the "noncommitment syndrome." We know how committed parents are to their children. The question is, what kind of a commitment does marriage involve?

Take a look at your hand for a moment, and ask yourself: How committed are you to your hand? The answer is — very committed. If a person has an accident and his hand is severely injured, and the doctor tells this person that in order to regain 90 to 95 percent usage of his hand he'll have to have a series of operations along with a long and difficult period of rehabilitation, is there any chance the person will say, "Forget it, Doc. It's too much. Just take the whole hand off"?

When the Torah describes the commitment of a husband and a wife to one another, it says, "and they shall become like one flesh" (Genesis 2:24). The commitment of a husband and a wife to one another is at least as deep as your commitment to your hand. In Judaism, through marriage, a man and a woman become one. Marriage is the transformation of two individuals into a new reality where they have a new, shared being. This is what is meant by becoming one. And it is based on commitment and loyalty.

Principle 3: Giving. Remember that the word *ahavah* (love) means "giving." There is another dimension to this word. Each letter of the Hebrew alphabet and each Hebrew word has a corresponding numerical value, called its *gematria*. The *gematria* of the letter *alef* is 1, *beis* is 2, *gimmel* is 3, *dalet* is 4, and so on. The *gematria* of the word *ahavah* is 13, the same numerical value as the Hebrew word *echad*, which means "one." According to the Jewish mystical system called Kabbalah, when two words have the same numerical value, it means the words have the same underlying meaning. Therefore, giving and oneness are equivalent. Giving leads to oneness.

Principle 4: Soul. Marriage is the most fertile ground there is for giving. On the deepest spiritual plane, marriage is the fusion of two people — two souls — into one. On the everyday plane, marriage provides us with the opportunity to develop our own inner beauty by giving to our spouse and thereby creating oneness in its deepest sense.

Once we begin to think about how profoundly deep love through giving can be, it becomes clear how much loftier, how much more meaningful it is than physical pleasure. Unlike the latter, love is based on a complex set of emotional, psychological, and spiritual interconnections that are rooted in the concept of giving. Because love is based on much more than physical pleasure, it is infinitely more rewarding.

Home Run Tips

- Love is a function of the relationship. The deeper the love, the deeper and closer the relationship will be. If one party loves less deeply than the other, the quality of the relationship will be only as strong as the person who loves the other less deeply wants it to be.

- When I say "I love you" to my spouse, what am I really saying? Am I saying that I am there for her emotionally and spiritually and that I give of myself to her to help her fulfill her destiny? Or do I love the fact that I have a perpetual date, that she provides for me, and that she makes me feel good? Is the focus of my love what I do for her, or what she does for me? If I were to be really honest with myself, I would have to admit that the focus is me. I love me. And I love how my significant other makes *me* feel. This, I believe, is one of the reasons why relationships often get stuck at a relatively superficial level. Too often we are focused on ourselves, as opposed to the other, and how deep can a self-centered relationship really be?

Rabbi Eliyahu Dessler, widely regarded as one of the great Jewish thinkers of the twentieth century, says that the more we give, the more we love. And the reason for this, he explains, is because the more we give, the more we become one with the recipient of our act of giving. Every act of giving is like planting a bit of ourselves in another.

Being kind, giving, and nurturing to acquaintances and friends is a lot easier than being consistently giving and nurturing to those closest to us. When we deal with our closest relationships, our own ego gets involved. The true test of our character comes when we can control our ego and be humble in our relationships. Being consistently good to those closest to us while asking nothing in return is being a real giver.

Chapter Eight
A Triple: Integrity — the Challenge of Being a Good Person

There are two famous Pulitzer Prize–winning images you might have seen. One photograph was taken during the Vietnam War. It shows a Vietnamese child holding onto her mother as they cross a rain-swollen, rushing river, seeking safety. The second photo is of a Biafran child suffering from severe malnutrition, with an ugly vulture perched nearby...waiting.

Behind every picture there is a hidden story. After taking the photo in Vietnam, the photographer helped the family reach safety. Years later, after the war, she went back to Vietnam and actually tracked down the woman in the picture and shared the prize money with her. The photographer in Biafra was deluged with mail once he returned to the States asking if, after taking the photo, he did anything to help that poor starving child. His answer was that the child was just one of thousands in that same situation, and so what could he do? People were horrified by his response, and he eventually committed suicide.

Now imagine if Timothy McVeigh and Mother Teresa were to walk into this room right now. Let us present the following question to both of them: Do you believe that you are a good person? Which of the two would have a harder time saying, "Yes, I believe that I am a good person" and which of the two would be more likely to hem and haw and say something like, "To be honest, I'm trying to be good, but I know how far short I have fallen of my goal"?

It is likely that Timothy McVeigh, the Oklahoma City bomber, would think, or thought, that he was a good person. He had no remorse over his crime and believed he was doing the right thing to bring America to justice. And it is likely that Mother Teresa would struggle with the question of just how good she really is. She might acknowledge or recognize inside that she is good, but nonetheless, it would be an ongoing struggle for her. She would probably have said that she could be better.

We have now discovered an interesting phenomenon. The closer someone is to the "good" of the human spectrum, the more unsure he will be about his own goodness. And the closer someone is to being evil, the more sure he will be that he is good. So how do we really define "good"?

Timothy McVeigh will rationalize his evil act. The question is, why? Rationalization is what goes on inside our heads when we are about to do, or have already done, something that we know is wrong. The confrontation with doing the wrong thing presents us with two basic choices. Either we can admit that it is wrong and deal with it as such, or we can rationalize. In other words, we can find some way to say that what we know is wrong, really isn't. Through rationalization, wrong suddenly becomes right. Or, if it's not exactly right, then there are at least very valid and "understandable" reasons why we did the wrong thing.

Rationalization is liberating; it lets us have our cake and eat it, too. Rationalization enables us to do the wrong thing and kind of gloss over it, find some way to fit it into the category of being right or good, and thereby continue to live in harmony with our deep desire to do good and be good. In other words, it allows us to continue living with ourselves.

Would you like to do business with someone who lacked integrity? Integrity is one of those cornerstone values in life that, if lacking, can bring down the whole foundation of an institution, whether that institution is a marriage, a friendship, a business partnership or a presidency. What exactly is this thing we call "integrity"?

Let's take a look at the four-step hierarchy of life according to Rabbi Chaim Vital, who quotes Rabbi Yitzchak Luria, the great kabbalist of the sixteenth century:

Domem — inanimate objects, like stones and soil
Tzomei'ach — plant life
Chai — animal life
Medaber — the speaker (man)

Why is man called "the speaker" rather than the "thinker" or the "one who reasons"? Isn't it man's ability to reason and to think intelligently that so clearly distinguishes him from animals? As Rene Descartes said, "I think; therefore, I am." Isn't thinking at least as much a distinction as speaking? Or how about distinguishing man in spiritual or emotional terms? Why not focus on the uniqueness of the human soul, or the uniquely rich and deep emotional life that human beings enjoy?

The difference between the power of speech and the other human capacities — thinking, feeling, possessing a soul — is that they are all internal processes. When we speak, we project our inner selves outward. Speech, the quintessential form of communication, is how my thoughts, my feelings, my inner self are projected outward to others. In classical Jewish thought, we analyze human behavior as beginning with thought, then moving to speech, and then proceeding to action.

Now let us factor into this equation the value of integrity. Integrity is the honest projection of one's thoughts through speech, which ultimately find expression in the form of deeds and action. To think, feel, and believe one thing and *say* another is the opposite of integrity. Similarly, to think, feel, and believe one thing and *do* another is the opposite of integrity.

The English word for integrity comes from the Latin word "integras," which means "wholeness." A person of integrity is a person whose speech and action are in sync — they reflect the entirety or wholeness of the individual's thoughts, speech, and deeds. It's not just what they say or do for public consumption; it's what they actually are on the inside as well. In the words of the Talmud, a person must be *tocho k'varo*, one's internal self must match one's external behavior. That is a person of integrity (Talmud Tractate *Berachos* 28a).

It's sad, but often, the people who are best known for their lack of integrity in our society are politicians, particularly when they are in the middle of an election campaign. It often seems like they will say or do almost anything, regardless of what they really think and feel, just to get our votes. Ironically, the system we have for choosing people to represent us often devolves into a kind of popularity contest that militates against candidates maintaining their integrity. The result is that we often have people representing us who have jettisoned their integrity for the right to be our representatives.

Based on this definition of integrity, Timothy McVeigh, incredibly, appears to be a man of integrity. McVeigh never hesitated to say that he was an anarchist and that he wanted to overthrow the American government. And eventually, he didn't hesitate to act upon what he thought and felt.

So I ask you, was Timothy McVeigh a man of integrity? Are the Al-Qaida terrorists, who say and believe that America is evil and who then proceed to act upon their convictions with terror, people of integrity because their speech matches their actions? Surely not. So there is obviously something wrong with our definition of integrity. What is the missing piece in our definition of integrity that would exclude Timothy McVeigh and Al-Qaida terrorists?

Let's revisit our view of morality. Imagine that two lives are in grave danger, and you can save only one. The first life is that of a mentally retarded child, and the second is the last blue whale on earth. Which life would you save?

The real question is this: Is there really a right or a wrong answer to this question, or is it just a matter of opinion? Meaning, even if all of us agreed that the child should be saved, would we be justified in condemning someone who chose to save the blue whale over the child? Or are they as entitled to their opinion as we are? To me that is one of the most, if not *the* most important, question every human being has to deal with, and ultimately, the fate of all mankind may lie in how people resolve this question.

A story was reported in the *Wall Street Journal* about a professor who received a paper from a student in his philosophy course defending moral relativism. The professor gave the student a D. The student was shocked by the grade and approached the professor to find out what was wrong with his paper. The professor said there was absolutely nothing wrong with the paper. The logic, the organization, and the sources were fine. If that was the case, the student wanted to know, "Why did I get a D?"

The professor said, "Because that's what I felt like giving you."

The student was outraged and demanded that his grade be changed. After all, he argued, it was wrong to base a grade on nothing more than the professor's personal whim. The professor protested, "But you yourself just wrote a beautiful paper arguing that there is no such thing as absolute right or wrong, and to me there's nothing wrong with giving out grades based on feelings rather than content." The student got the point, and the professor changed his grade to an A.

Deep down, we all want to believe that morality is objective. Otherwise, there is no moral compass to live by. We have this need for direction and guidance. (That is why children crave rules and boundaries. They need it for their sense of existential security.) Ultimately, though, we cannot prove that morality is objective. It is a question of faith. But it does not matter that it cannot be proven. We do know that it is simply not a matter of opinion whether euthanasia is okay. It is not a matter of opinion whether handicapped children should be left to die. It is not a matter of opinion whether we should allow the concept of the survival of the fittest to govern decisions as to who receives medical services. We know deep down that these questions are not within the purview of our opinions. There is a true answer to these questions, and that truth ultimately comes from a Source that transcends the subjectivity of the human mind and psyche.

In the absence of objective morality, all moral decisions are reduced to the level of the choice between Baskin-Robbins ice cream flavors. Some people like chocolate, some like vanilla, and others prefer Pralines 'N Cream. Similarly, some people like stealing, some like healing, and others like a scoop of each. Some like children, some like whales — and some would save baby whales but not adult ones.

During the American Civil War, the Mason-Dixon Line between Pennsylvania and Maryland was the dividing line between the North and South, between good and evil. You see, in one of the oddest phenomena in all of American history, all the "bad" people — slaveholders, that is — just happened to live south of the Mason-Dixon Line, while all the "good" people — those who opposed slavery — lived north of that line.

The Mason-Dixon Line illustrates that what I consider to be right or good — in other words, my moral views — usually corresponds to what's right or good for my stomach. Why so? The reason the South chose to support slavery was that its economy

— plantation farming — depended on slavery. And the residents of the North were able to oppose slavery because their economy was industrialized and did not need slaves to survive. There was no magic in the Mason-Dixon Line that divided all the moral people into the North and all the immoral racists into the South. Their moral stance merely followed their economies.

If what's right, good, and moral isn't just a matter of opinion, then what is it a matter of? The Jewish understanding is that morality can't come from within us; it can only come from a Source that transcends *all* of us. Since we are all subject to our own needs, interests, and stomachs, we can't help but be subjective when making decisions about things that affect us. Judaism understands that what's right in life derives from the transcendent Source of all life. In other words, it's not up to you or I to decide who to save — the child or the blue whale — rather, the Creator of the child, the whale, *and you and me*, has the sole right to determine morality.

Only in a world where God determines morality can there ever be a universal ban on murder — and outrage at genocide — that is *absolutely* true and credible. If there is any other arbiter of morality, then we are left with a world governed according to pragmatic, utilitarian values, the law of the jungle, where might makes right, or the whims of someone's personal tastes and preferences dictate the rules.

We have now solved the problem of Timothy McVeigh and Al-Qaida terrorists being men of integrity. They are not. The reason is that there is more to integrity than the honest projection outward of one's thoughts and convictions through speech and action. If the definition of integrity is "someone who honestly speaks his mind," then he can have integrity but still be a moral monster. The thoughts, beliefs, and convictions that make up one's inner world must ultimately be rooted in a higher, transcendent world, a world of absolute truth. Only if our inner world and values are anchored in the spiritual world can there truly be integrity. So here is our new definition of integrity: the projection outward of a Godly and spiritual inner self in the form of speech and action that corresponds to that standard of Godly morality.

One last question about rationalization: Why do we rationalize? Why can't we just see fit to call a spade a spade and say to ourselves, "I know that what I am about to do is wrong, and frankly, I don't care." Why do we put ourselves through all the trouble of trying to come up with all sorts of elaborate rationalizations when we could do something much easier — tell the truth: I'm bad, I did bad, I'll continue to do what's bad, and who cares? It's my life, and I can be as bad as I want.

The reason we don't just take the easy way out is because it would be too painful. Our desire to be good is such a central part of our being that the pain of having to look at ourselves as being anything other than good drives us to rationalize. It seems that an inclination toward conscience is hardwired into our psyche. In other words, we are driven to integrity, and if we don't have it, we'll rationalize it away to maintain a spiritual equilibrium — to be able to live with ourselves.

The bottom line is that our desire to be good and our desire for integrity are one and the same. And both, ultimately, are rooted in a desire to transcend ourselves and be connected to the ultimate Source of good, the ultimate Source of spirituality: God. We've now hit a triple and we're standing on third base.

But what about love — and standing on second base? Isn't love the most powerful thing on earth? How could integrity be a more powerful drive than love? Let's consider *Casablanca*, arguably the best movie ever made. Rick, an American living in Paris, fell in love with a woman named Ilsa, who thought her husband had died at the hands of the Nazis in World War II. Then Ilsa's husband showed up alive in Paris — he was actually fighting with the underground partisans against the Nazis. Rick had planned to escape the war with two exit visas that he had procured — one for himself and one for Ilsa. He arranged to meet Ilsa at the airport for their flight to freedom, but instead he gave the two visas to Ilsa and her husband. He told Ilsa that her husband needed her by his side, since he was fighting for true freedom, against tyranny. And so Rick showed that integrity takes precedence over love — it is a higher motivation for living.

Let's conclude this chapter with an analogy. Electricity from a power plant can flow into the house only if the light switch is turned on. Think of God as the power plant, as the ultimate power source. Think of yourself as a lightbulb. And think of the world as a dark room. The light switch, that's integrity. When we are able to recognize the reality of objective morality — which is God — and when we are able to express and project that Godliness into the world, which is acting with integrity, then we are all capable of becoming meaningful sources of light in what is often a very dark world.

Home Run Tips 𝙭

◑ If morality is relative, then there is no morality. There is either an objective determinant of right and wrong — something other than personal opinion or self-interest — or there is no such thing as right and wrong at all. All we would be left with is merely equally valid opinions.

◑ Even though our liberal sense of justice inclines us to believe that everyone is entitled to his own sense of truth, in reality we are all too tied to our own needs, desires, and inclinations to determine right from wrong on our own. The only way to get at absolute morality and truth is to become aware that they have to come from a transcendent source — which most monotheistic faiths believe was Mount Sinai — the Ten Commandments as revealed by the Transcendent Source. When we strive to understand, study, and aspire to the standards of that absolute truth, then we have achieved integrity.

Chapter Nine

A Home Run: Creating a Legacy and Making Your Mark — the Power of Making a Difference

I magine either or both of the following scenarios:

Scenario 1: You have a friend who has been working in cancer research for the last ten years who comes to you with the following dilemma. She says, "I am 90 percent convinced that I will have a cure for cancer within the next five to ten years, but there is a problem, and I need your advice. I know that the intensity of the work required will be such that I will have virtually no time for myself or my family. I'll be working incredibly long hours, and even when I'm not working, I'll need to be constantly on call. What do you think I should do? Do you think it's worth the sacrifice?"

Scenario 2: You are contacted by the White House. You are provided with a date, time, and location for a meeting. You are in
shock when you realize that at this meeting are none other than
the president of the United States, the vice president, and all
the other living former presidents and vice presidents. Additionally, you are introduced, one by one, to the secretary-general
of the United Nations, the head of the European Union, the
presidents of Russia and China, as well as the pope, the Dalai
Lama, and the chief rabbis of Israel.

The Dalai Lama speaks to you on behalf of the assembled
and says: "You have been chosen to act on behalf of this group
to carry out the most important mission any of us has ever un-
dertaken. We have been meeting in secret for the last five years
and have devised what we believe to be the best plan for achieving world peace. There is just one problem with our plan: It can
only be carried out by someone other than ourselves, and after
great research, we have decided that you are the person." Will
you do it?

If your friend in scenario 1 and you in scenario 2 accepted
these assignments, would you say that it would make their respective parents happy? I would say so. In fact, all that parents
really want is a little *nachas*, delight, from their children.

Beyond being financially successful, parents basically want
two things for their children: they want them to be happy, and
they want them to be good. All the wealth in the world isn't
worth very much if a person isn't happy. The same with being a
good, decent, moral person. What good is all the money in the
world if a person isn't a decent human being? For parents, good,
happy children are the cake; wealth is just the icing. But beyond
wealth, there is an even sweeter dessert for parents.

Imagine the feelings of a parent who could say, "My daughter
is such a fine woman, such a good, caring person...*and*...thanks
to her research, babies no longer die of malnutrition in Africa,"
or "Thanks to her, there is now a cure for cancer," or "Thanks

to her, one thousand children per year from poor homes get to attend summer camps," or "Thanks to her, there is peace in Somalia," or (this one will qualify her for being the Messiah) "Thanks to her, there is peace between Israel and the Arabs."

Isn't it obvious that on the parental-*nachas* meter, these achievements give a parent a whole different level of pleasure? What is it about these achievements that are so wonderful?

The answer is that beyond being good (which is an enormous and invaluable achievement, one that can't be undervalued), these people have added to the overall good of the world. They have gone beyond themselves and made a difference for others as well.

How can one make a difference and leave a legacy in the world? Here are some strategies and tools:

The Hebrew word for power is *memshalah*. Israelis use the word *memshalah* to mean "government" or "the seat of power." "Power," however, is a loaded word. It has all sorts of negative connotations, connotations that were immortalized in 1887 by the words of the British Lord John Acton when he wrote in a letter to Bishop Mandell Creighton that "Power tends to corrupt, and absolute power corrupts absolutely."

Let's take another look at politicians, and this time, let's give them a reasonable benefit of the doubt. People go into politics because they want to make a contribution to their community, their city, or their country. They are well-meaning, idealistic people who want to make a difference. Unfortunately, they don't always stay that way. What happens to politicians along the way that causes them to jettison the values and principles they started out with? Why is it that the very people who begin careers with the good of others in mind frequently end up being derided for being concerned about little more than themselves? We all know that if our society is cynical about anyone, it's cynical about politicians.

Let me put it another way. If the drive for integrity, the drive to be a good person, is so strong that it trumps the drive for love, then what is it that could possibly trump the drive for integrity? If we look at our hierarchy of hits in a baseball game, the answer becomes clear: Power is a home run, and there is something seductive about home runs. The pleasure of power is so intense that it can seduce even the finest people into compromising what made them such good people in the first place. When Lord Acton said that power corrupts, he was commenting on the seductive allure that power holds.

Does this mean that good people should stay away from politics? That would be unfortunate, wouldn't it? After all, government does have the potential to exert a positive influence on society and to improve people's lives, so it would be a shame if good people were discouraged from getting involved.

Power corrupts because it's a cheap thrill. Let us illustrate with an example. There are two ways a woman can own a diamond necklace: either she can spend thousands on the real thing, or, if she can't afford the real thing, she can spend just hundreds and buy a very nice faux diamond necklace. The downside of this kind of jewelry is that it's not real. The upside is that you get at least some of the pleasure of owning a diamond necklace. Power, at least the corruptive and destructive power we are used to thinking of, is a faux experience. It's an illusion of something more profound, more real. Real power is creativity. Genuine, authentic creativity is the ability to build, to create something that projects and promotes goodness into the world. Genuine power then is the power to create and build. It's a power hitter hitting a home run.

Imagine you were able to bring peace to the Middle East. What an incredible feeling of accomplishment, what an enormous difference that would make for so many and for the world. What a feeling of creative power that would generate! That is what power does when it is wedded to integrity, morality, and what is good and right. So the power of leaving a legacy in the world is based on principles of integrity. It is not that making your mark in the world is better than integrity; rather, it incorporates integrity and brings it home. But power for power's sake — that's destruction. And it is easier to destroy than to build. It's always easier to create a faux experience, whether it's faux jewelry, a forged piece of art, or counterfeit dollar bills, than it is to create and earn the real thing.

The Jewish view of *memshalah*, power, is about building. It's about using one's abilities to create and build in the service of one's morality and integrity. That's real power, and that's a highly pleasurable sense of meaning — a real home run, not a virtual home run.

It's interesting to note that in Judaism, the essence of kingship is not to rule or to legislate, but to be a provider for the nation. Historically, certainly at the time when the Jewish people actually had a king and throughout most of history since then, a king was little more than a great exploiter — the polar opposite of the Jewish idea. By and large, kings have taken the resources of others to serve themselves. Only from the time of the French Revolution some two hundred years ago was that idea seriously challenged.

Judaism asserts that everyone has the power of true *memshalah* — the ability to make a difference. Think of a person who has had a lasting and positive influence on your life, someone of whom you could say, "Thanks to him or her, my life is much different than it may have been, and in a very good way." Why not take a moment and write that person a letter or give him a call? Appreciation will give both of you a sense of fulfillment. He has used his power in a creative way to make a difference in your life.

The Torah gives us an insight into how God intended that man make a difference. The Talmud asks why Adam, the first human being, was created alone. At the time of his creation he had no wife, no family, no neighbors — he was a lone human being. The Talmud's answer is that Adam was created alone so that he would experience looking at the world as an individual and say to himself, "The world was created for me" (Talmud Tractate *Sanhedrin* 38a).

What do these words mean? A child's understanding of "The world was created for me" is that it's all mine and I can do whatever I want with it. In fact, children often think that because a toy is theirs, they have the right to neglect and destroy it as they see fit. After all, they say, "You got the toy for me. It's mine, and I can do whatever I want with it." Or they feel that they don't need to share it with their siblings or neighbors because "It's mine!" An adult, on the other hand, knows that when something is his it means he is responsible for it.

The Jewish understanding is that Adam was created alone so that he would feel the world was his, not to destroy, but to take care of and to safeguard. Adam was given a twofold responsibility in the Garden of Eden, to care for the garden and to safeguard it from harm: "*l'avdah u'leshamrah* — to work it and to guard it" (Genesis 2:15). This means that we are all symbolically Adam. Every human being is responsible for the well-being of the entire world. That's an incredible statement about human potential and human power — the creative kind.

One way of looking at early history as depicted in the Torah is as the history of personal responsibility.

Adam: Adam was instructed not to eat from the tree of knowledge, but he did. When God confronted him, not only did Adam not take responsibility for what he had done, but he laid the blame on God for having given him Eve, as the Torah says: "The woman whom *You* gave to me, she gave to me and I ate" (Genesis 3:12). What does that say about man's natural response to God's challenge? Blame someone else!

Cain: Cain killed his brother, Abel, not a nice thing to do. While his action was horrible, when confronted, at least he didn't blame someone else for what he did. He didn't try to say that he was the product of a bad family environment, that the other kids in school goaded him into doing what he did, that he was a latchkey child, that he had too much junk food growing up and it scrambled his brain, or anything like that. At the same time, he didn't take responsibility for his actions. When God asked him where Abel was, Cain answered: "Am I my brother's keeper?" (Genesis 4:9). That isn't exactly an example of being ready to assume responsibility for one's actions.

Noah: Now here's a guy who was ready to accept responsibility, at least for himself and his family. He built an ark to save his family. When it came to the rest of the world, however, Noah really didn't do enough.

Abraham: Now we're talking responsibility. When God told Abraham that He was going to destroy the city of Sodom, Abraham immediately jumped to its defense and tried to do whatever he could to get God to spare the people of Sodom. And these people weren't exactly angels, either.

Let's analyze this. Noah ended up saving mankind from the flood. Abraham became the founding father of the Jewish people, a people that would impact all of mankind with its belief in one God and its resultant belief in one universal standard of behavior for all men. The question is, why wasn't Noah, who was a thoroughly righteous man (Genesis 6:9) and who ended up being chosen by God as the one through whom mankind would be saved and rebuilt, chosen to be the father of the Jewish people? After all, if the mission of the Jewish people is to be a blessing and make a difference to humanity, then why isn't the person who merited to save humanity in the first place chosen to be the father of that mission?

The Torah commentators outline a significant distinction between Noah and Abraham. While Noah was a righteous man, never once did he make an effort to draw others closer to God. He wasn't prepared to take responsibility for people and the world around him. Noah did not walk around in the days preceding the flood and ask people to improve their ways. He did not hold seminars on spirituality and self-improvement. Abraham, on the other hand, devoted himself to trying to have an impact on others. He and his wife, Sarah, taught others about

God. He had the chutzpah to argue with God in order to try to save the people of Sodom and Gomorrah. Abraham was a man of responsibility, and that is what enabled him to become the cornerstone of the Jewish people, a nation that would ultimately be charged with nothing less than being "a light unto the nations" (Isaiah 60:2–3).

We have looked at the difference between two great men, Noah and Abraham. Now we are going to look at the two largest construction projects in the Torah. The first is the infamous Tower of Babel, and the second is the Tabernacle in the desert, which later became the centerpiece of the Temple in Jerusalem.

In the story of the Tower of Babel (Genesis 11:4), which we all remember from Hebrew school, the people wanted to "reach up to the heavens" — which sounds like a good thing. The problem is that they wanted to reach the heavens in order to do battle with God. If that were really the case and these people were so primitive that they thought God lived in the heavens, then where should they have built their tower? On a mountain, of course. Where did they build it? In a valley.

What they were really saying was this: We can build a city — a society, here in this valley — without God. We will do battle with God by excluding Him from our lives. After all, we are intelligent, sophisticated professionals. We don't need God to build a community. We can make for ourselves a "name" and forget about the Name of God.

What did God have to say about this self-sufficient, self-serving building project? He said: Try to get along without a common language — a common bond that is brought about by Me, the unifying Force and Source of the universe. So God mixed up their languages. They could not build the tower, and their project failed.

And then there was the other great building project: the Tabernacle in the desert after the Jewish people came out of Egypt. It was to house the Ten Commandments they received on Mount Sinai and serve as a symbol of God's presence in their midst. This project succeeded because the people were humble enough to realize that they could not build a society without the Great Unifier, God. With the Tower of Babel, the people wanted to make a "name for themselves" (Genesis 11:4), whereas with the Tabernacle, the people wanted to make a name and a place for God in their lives. That, in essence, is the difference between corrupted power and truly creative power.

The Tower of Babel is an example of human beings using their abilities to build a city and a skyscraper of unprecedented magnitude. Employing the vastness of human potential in the service of such a project was potentially a wonderful thing. However, since its motivation was egocentric, since it was meant to bear testimony to the power of man, its end was destruction. Power for the sake of self is power for power's sake, and that is destructive. Power for the sake of making a name for God and spirituality is ultimate creativity. When the power of human potential and capability is harnessed toward spirituality, one is capable of building a structure that can make the ultimate difference — it can bring an awareness of God into the world.

What we have discovered here is the deepest spiritual dimension of what the Jewish people are all about, and, ultimately, what each of our lives is about. The story of the Jewish people begins with a man named Abraham, who undertook the responsibility of not only leading a spiritual life but of helping others do the same. Eventually, the people who came out of this one man, his wife, and their family would be called upon to implement the most creative endeavor human beings could ever undertake, namely, the creation of a means for God to be manifest in the world, and for all of mankind to be aware of His presence and His standards. In the Jewish way of thinking, this is ultimate creativity, this is what power looks like when it is channeled, and this is the key to being a "light unto the nations."

I know what you are thinking: "Can I really make a difference in the world? I'm just one person, and making a difference seems so overwhelming." To this the Talmud has an answer: The Talmud says, "Whoever saves one life is as if he saved an entire world (Talmud Tractate *Sanhedrin* 37a). The Jewish idea is that every individual is like a microcosm of the entire world. While this is a concept with deep and even mystical meanings and ramifications, suffice it to say that to make a difference in the life of just one person is an accomplishment of enormous meaning and import.

Every human being is charged with creating a legacy in the world. According to Judaism, everyone has a place and a role to play in God's world. A Jew gets to where he needs to go by performing the 613 Torah commandments, and a non-Jew gets there by performing the seven Noachian laws that were given to Adam and Eve (they got six) and to Noah (he got a seventh). These seven laws encompass the entirety of living a decent and fulfilled life:

1. **Believe in One God** — go by one standard of behavior and decency

2. **Do not curse God** — make it a theocentric, not an egocentric world

3. **Do not murder** — respect the sanctity of human life

4. **Do not commit adultery** — respect the ultimate human relationship

5. **Do not steal** — respect the division of property

6. **Make a civil law system to adjudicate disputes** — respect society

7. **Do not tear a limb off a live animal and eat it** — respect and have sensitivity for animal life

So in Judaism it is not just the Jew who gets to serve God. Everyone does. And therefore, everyone is given the opportunity to make a difference in God's world.

Let me share an example of how one man can make a difference. Marvin Berlin started with one carpet store and eventually built a billion-dollar business with a chain of hundreds of stores across the country. One of his most successful salesmen was suspected of embezzling money from the company, and it turned out he had a gambling problem. When Marvin called the man into his office, he knew the gig was up. Marvin stared at the man across from him for what seemed to be an eternity and said, "How can I help? What can I do to get you out of this mess?" That moment changed the man's life and the life of his family. With the help and support of Marvin Berlin he was able to beat his addiction to gambling, an addiction that nearly destroyed him, his career, his marriage, and his family.

People's lives have ups and downs, just like the waxing and waning of the moon. And it is no coincidence that the Jewish calendar is governed by the moon, as opposed to the Gregorian calendar, which is a solar calendar. In fact, the very first commandment that was given to the Jewish people as a nation after they left Egypt was the commandment to establish the moon as the basis for the Jewish calendar (see Exodus 12:2). God's first commandment to the Jewish people wasn't to observe Shabbos, keep kosher, or even to believe in One God. It was rather to be aware of the moon, keep track of its cycles, and celebrate holidays based on witnessing the new moon and its stages.

In terms of creativity, and the spirituality of creativity, the moon represents two things: First, the moon is reflective. Though it has no real light of its own, it is a great source of light. The moon is devoted to projecting the sun's light and is thus capable of channeling that light. The moon, in its humility, harnesses all of its power to reflect the rays of the sun. The Jewish people, like the moon, are a source of light, reflective light. Our potential as a people, and as individuals, is to use all of our abilities — all of our power from God — in order to reflect a higher light.

Second, the moon is a model for making a difference and becoming a light. Every new month in the Jewish calendar begins with the appearance of the first sliver of a new moon. From there, it grows and grows each day until it's a bright full moon on the fourteenth and fifteenth night of the Jewish month. This is a model for making a difference. You don't have to try to become a full moon overnight. You begin by making a "small" difference, a difference even with yourself, then perhaps a difference with some friends and then perhaps with your community. The point is that making a difference can be a gradual process.

Additionally, the moon tells us never to give up. Even though every full moon eventually begins to wane until there is nothing left, that's not really what's taking place. It's just getting ready to begin shining again. In this way the moon gives us a sense of hope that we can renew ourselves even after we "disappear" in a difficulty or crisis.

Let's conclude this chapter with a story. It's the story of a Swedish manufacturer and inventor who lived in Stockholm during the last half of the nineteenth century, Alfred Bernhard Nobel (1833–1896). Alfred Nobel became a very wealthy man because of one invention, dynamite. However, at the end of his life, Mr. Nobel decided that he didn't want his legacy to be that of a person who created a means to safely and efficiently destroy things, so in his will he left nine million dollars to establish six Nobel Prizes, in physics, chemistry, physiology, medicine, literature, and peace. Today, Alfred Nobel is known to the world not for the invention that made him a wealthy man, but because of the achievements of others.

Mr. Nobel stood for the idea that if you want to create a legacy, a name for yourself in the world, the best way to do it is by helping others and helping the world. And who knows? By helping others, your legacy might become a legacy of peace.

Now let's review our baseball model and see where we are up to in winning the game of life:

Single — physical pleasure

Double — love

Triple — integrity

Home run — creating a legacy

Now let's move on to the deepest level and explore the ultimate, how to win the game. The way to do that is to put all these hits into the perspective of a truly meaningful life, which is a life dedicated to spirituality. And let's do that by getting into the finer aspects of Jewish spirituality.

Home Run Tips 𝓧

- To be a good person, a person of integrity, is a deep pleasure that gives a strong sense of meaning and inner contentment, but beware of power — because power can go to our heads and distract us from our initial noble intentions.

- The Jewish people stand for the idea of making a difference. They are charged with creating a spiritual legacy for the world. If you are Jewish, when you do a mitzvah — like giving charity (*tzedakah*), lighting Chanukah candles on Chanukah, keeping kosher, or anything Jewish — you are adding another brick to the great edifice of Jewish legacy.

Chapter Ten

Hit and Run: Building a Community with Kindness

The batter gets to first base with a single. The manager may decide to move the runner along to advance into scoring position, so he may call on the next batter and runner, who is now at first base, to perform a "hit and run." On a given pitch the runner on first base breaks for second base as if he is attempting to steal second base, and the hitter must swing at and hit the ball, even if it is outside the strike zone. The batter tries to hit the ball "behind" the runner, that is, to the right side of the infield, in order to make it harder for the fielders to turn a double play. Hopefully, the ball will "split" the infield and find a hole between first base and second base, and both runners will be safe.

The manager may call for the hit and run instead of a sacrifice bunt because the batter may be a good hitter and the runner a fast runner, and he may not want to go for a guaranteed out at first, as is the case with a sacrifice bunt. He may want the hitter and runner, who are well suited for this type of play, to "go for it" and try to get both the new batter and the current runner on first base to get a rally going or to keep up his team's momentum.

The precision required to execute the hit and run is akin to the hit and run that my children and I perform every Thursday night and which is repeated in tens of communities around the world. I take my kids to a special warehouse on Thursday nights where we meet twenty other volunteers who are stuffing boxes with sugar, flour, pasta, bread, and other staples. Once the boxes are filled, each volunteer is given a piece of paper with five addresses on it and is asked to deliver the food boxes to those addresses. There are no names on the papers, just addresses, in order to protect the recipients' identity and thus save them the embarrassment of knowing that others know they need food packages. My children help me carry the box up to the home, and then, in a carefully coordinated operation, I go back to the car to get it started while one of the children knocks on the door and the other children make a mad dash for the car to avoid being seen by the recipients of this charity box. The knock on the door is the "hit" and the undetected escape is the "run."

The reason for this hit and run is that we make great efforts to spare the recipients of charity embarrassment. This is an example of sensitivity and is one of the highest form of charity. I say "one of the highest forms" because there is a higher level of giving — when neither the giver not the recipient know each other. In other words, when one gives charity anonymously, that is guaranteed to protect the recipient from embarrassment, and hence, it is a higher level of giving.

Notice that giving charity is not merely a nice thing to do. It is a mitzvah, a Torah obligation. There are 613 such Torah mitzvos, or obligations. We are obligated to help others, since they are our brothers and sisters. And the obligation aspect is not merely so that the poor shall be looked after. Maimonides suggests that if you have a hundred dollars to give to charity, you should give one dollar to a hundred different needy people rather than giving a hundred dollars to one person. Why? Because when you put your hand in your pocket one hundred times, you transform your character into a giving personality, which is much more growth producing than the single act of giving a one hundred dollar donation. Thus, charity is not only about what it does for the needy; it is also about what it does for the giver. Giving charity changes a person's essence. It transforms him into a charitable person (Maimonides' eight levels of charity, *Yad HaChazakah*, "Laws of Gifts to the Poor," 10:1, 7–14).

In the early 1900s a saintly rabbi named Rabbi Yisrael Meir Kagan of Radin, Poland, also known as the Chafetz Chaim, was asked for advice by a congregant: "I have been offered a job at the bank," the congregant told him. "Should I take a job as a deposit teller or a dispensing teller?" (In those days there was a bank teller for deposits and a different teller for withdrawals.) Rabbi Kagan answered that he should become a withdrawal teller so that he not become accustomed to taking money all day. And by giving out money all day he would become a more giving person.

We see, therefore, that the *chesed* (doing kind deeds) aspect of Jewish life is an organized and planned endeavor that must be coordinated and executed with precision and in a timely fashion. And the results are of benefit to the batter and the runner — the giver and the recipient. If God wanted to make the needy people in the community less needy or even wealthy, He could certainly do so. The Talmud says that a person is made to suffer poverty or wealth based on his God-given destiny, in order to test him and help him grow into the person he is supposed to become. The charity system, therefore, helps provide for the needs of the less fortunate while developing the character and personality of the givers.

A person's character development is called his *middos* development. Each person has to take an ongoing personal inventory of his character as he journeys through life. It is not the person with the most money who wins the game; it is the person who grew the most who merits the ultimate win — a place in the World to Come, the spiritual world we enter after we die.

Sir Moses Montefiore, an Orthodox Jew and philanthropist who lived in England in the nineteenth century, was once asked how much he was worth.

He answered, "I am worth forty thousand pounds."

"But you own millions in assets. How can you be worth only forty thousand pounds?" asked his friend.

Sir Moses replied, "You did not ask what I own. I own millions in assets and holdings. Rather, you asked what I am worth. I am worth the amount of charity I have given this year, and that is forty thousand pounds."

According to Jewish thought, a person's worth is not his net worth. The worth and worthiness of an individual is the amount of *chesed* — kind deeds and charitable activities — that he performs.

Home Run Tips 人

❧ According to Maimonides, the twelfth-century jurist, physician, and philosopher, the highest level of giving charity is where the recipient does not know from whom he is receiving the charity and the giver does not know to whom he is delivering it — all this to maintain the privacy and respect the feelings of the recipients, who may be embarrassed to have others know they are receiving charity. Thus, giving with dignity is part of the mitzvah of giving charity.

❧ In our society, the most often asked question when you meet someone new is: What do you do? People want to know in what social class you belong, so they ask the job or career question to size you up. In Jewish life, that is not the question that should be asked. The first question should be: What charitable activities are you involved in? That is an indication of a person's true worth.

Chapter Eleven
Sacrifice: Selflessness

There is a difference in baseball between a sacrifice fly and a sacrifice bunt. When a batter hits a long fly ball to the outfield and the ball is caught, any runner on base can "tag up" by staying on base until the ball is caught, and then the runner can advance to the next base, even from third base to home. This is called a sacrifice fly. The batter did not intend to get out. He intended to get a hit and drive the runner home. Still, even if the ball is caught, the batter is awarded an RBI, a run batted in, if the runner tags up at third and runs home safely. And if a runner advances to any other base, the batter is awarded a statistical award — a sacrifice — even though he was called out when the ball was caught.

There is another type of sacrifice, when there is a runner on base and the batter wants to advance the runner to put the team in a better scoring position. In this case, the batter purposely bunts the ball, knowing full well that he likely will be thrown out at first base. This is a real sacrifice, because he purposely gives up his chance at getting a hit, merely in order to advance the runner and help the team move closer to scoring a run. In fact, the sacrifice bunt is the manager's call. The manager instructs the batter to bunt and get out, and for his trouble he too is awarded a statistical "sacrifice," as he himself is called out at first base. The sacrifice bunt is more altruistic than the sacrifice fly, since the batter intends to sacrifice his place on base in the hopes of advancing the runner into scoring position and ultimately help the team win the game.

If we think about it, we could wonder why people voluntarily have children. Sleepless nights, cleaning up messes, working extra hours to pay school tuition when we would much rather be on vacation.... Does staying up till three in the morning wondering where your sixteen-year-old is with your car seem like your idea of a good time? The reason we choose to have children is because we want something greater than ourselves. We want to create and build something we can contribute to, share with, and give to.

Today's marketplace emphasizes being a team player and creating consensus. Businesses and even schools are emphasizing the cooperative model of profitability and success. The Talmud relates that there were five poor people in a bunk bed and they all shared one blanket (Tractate *Sanhedrin* 20a). If you have ever shared a blanket with someone, you will have experienced the "push-me-pull-you" tension about control over the blanket. The Talmud relates that they were able to share one blanket because each person pushed the blanket toward the next person. The underlying basis of sacrifice for another, then, is giving and becoming a charitable person. This leads to the development of values and growth in character.

In Judaism, there are two types of self-sacrifice. One is when a person is called upon to give up his life to show that God is more important than life itself. For example, Jewish law requires a person to allow himself to be killed rather than bow down to an idol in public, commit an adulterous act, or kill another human being. If someone puts a gun to your head and demands that you commit one of these three cardinal sins or be killed, then you are obligated to give up your life. This is called dying *al kiddush Hashem*, to sanctify God's Name. If we cross over certain red lines, we are sacrificing our spiritual lives anyway, so we must be willing to die rather than cross that red line. This is a sacrifice that is commanded by God. When people become martyrs because they are Jews, that is likewise considered dying *al kiddush Hashem*. Every Jew who was murdered in the Holocaust died *al Kiddush Hashem*, in sanctification of God's Name.

There is a second type of sacrifice that is more of a daily occurrence — sacrificing creature comforts to show a sense of dedication to *live*, rather than die, as a Jew. This is based on the Torah requirement of *"vachai bahem* — and you shall live by them" (Leviticus 18:5). We call it an act of *mesirus nefesh* (selfless dedication) to get out of bed on a cold winter morning to join a *minyan* (a quorum of ten men needed for congregational prayers) at synagogue, or to study Torah even though one is tired, or to organize a communal event to benefit others even though one derives no personal benefit from it. This is a selflessness that speaks to the high-level character of an individual who is willing to dedicate herself to others. When we act with this type of personal sacrifice we are like the hitter who bunts someone to second base even though he will be out at first base. To do that, to act in someone else's best interest rather than one's own, is to go against a basic motivation for living — the drive for self-preservation — and be willing to seek the advancement of others. Where does the strength to do that come from? It comes from getting in touch with one's inner soul — one's Godly self.

When we call God our "King," what do we mean? Do we imagine Him as a regal figure sitting on a royal throne in ermine robes, wearing a golden crown and carrying a scepter? These are symbols of royalty, but they are not the essence of kingship. In Jewish thought, we derive the definition of something from its function. The function of a king is to lead, rule, or legislate. But the main job of a king is to provide for his subjects. He supplies them with health care, police and fire protection, roads, and food. That is why we call God the King of kings — because He is the ultimate Provider of life itself.

When human beings act as providers to others, we become co-creators with God. We are acting regal or Godlike. When we act like God, we get closer to God. That is why King David says: "*Olam chesed yibaneh* — the world is built on acts of kindness" (Psalms 89:3).

The Torah says: "Make for Me a sanctuary so that I will dwell amongst them" (Exodus 25:8). Rashi, the eleventh-century Torah commentator, asks: Shouldn't the Torah say, Make Me a sanctuary so that I will dwell in *it*? Why does it say, "so that I will dwell amongst *them*?" Rashi answers that God does not dwell in buildings. He comes into this world and dwells in us — when we make our bodies, our psyches, and our lives into dwelling places for His presence. We do that by acting like God; by being givers and providers, to others.

To discover the essence of something, all you need to do is identify its purpose. The purpose of a plowshare is to till the land, so the essence of a plowshare, the definition of a plowshare, is a tool used to till the land. The purpose of a computer is to store and communicate information. So its essence is a tool of storage and communication.

What is man's essence? To answer that, we need to identify our purpose in the world. What is our purpose in being in this world? Many of us would answer: to be happy. That would be achieved by pursuing pleasure: Jacuzzis, steak, and vacations, as we discussed earlier. Is experiencing these sensual pleasures our purpose in life? Do we actually dedicate our lives to them? These pleasures are fleeting. Only something that is eternal can be our purpose, because purpose indicates an ultimate goal. And that which is fleeting and decays over time, like a good steak, cannot be eternal. Savoring a good steak, although highly pleasurable, cannot be our purpose in life.

Secondly, man's life purpose must, of necessity, give you a

sense of the "definition" of a human being. Does pleasure define us? Does the stimulation of our nerve endings define who we are? Purpose has to have a sense of destiny.

When you are having an argument with someone, it is so frustrating to try to convince him of your point of view, especially when you know that you are right and they just don't "get it." What if we went through our entire lives pursuing sensual pleasures, assuming that through them we would achieve happiness, since happiness is our life purpose...and then found out that we were wrong after all, that happiness is not the purpose of life. How would we feel if we missed the point of our entire lives?

Our true purpose, according to the Jewish system of winning the game of life, is to become the best person we can become — by acting like God. That is why man's name in the Torah is Adam, not Igor, Nigel, or Steven. Adam comes from the Hebrew word *adamah*, which means "ground," "clay," or "earth." We can serve our earthly natures by pursuing physical pleasures, or we can be *adameh*, which in Hebrew means "to be like (God)."

In *Pirkei Avos* (*Ethics of the Fathers*) 1:14, we find the famous statement by Hillel: "If I am not for myself, who will be for me? If I am only for myself, what am I? If not now, when?" The Maharal of Prague comments on man not being "only for himself" by bringing a parable about a farmer who marries a princess. The farmer tries to please the princess by bringing her freshly picked vegetables from the farm, taking her on wagon rides over the meadows, and plying her with delicious watermelons. But she is not impressed. She is used to the finer things in life — feasts at the palace, fine linen, and elegant state parties.

So, too, is it with the body and soul. The farmer in the story is the body. The princess is the soul. Our earthly body, which is made up of elements like potassium, sodium, calcium, carbon, and water, to name a few, cannot find fulfillment and satisfaction when we "feed" it with other physical elements, because

the soul is a princess; it is made of finer stuff. No physical deli-
cacy or pleasure can bring true happiness to the soul. The soul,
a piece of God that He breathed into us, can be fulfilled only
with things that touch the princess in ourselves — our eternal
nature. When a person acts Godlike by giving to others, then
the soul connects with its Godly Source. This is called *deveikus*,
joining with God.

Home Run Tips 🏃

◈ Would you rather receive or give a gift? When we
receive a gift, we feel happy because we are being
noticed and appreciated. It builds our sense of worth
and value. I suggest that the feeling of contentment
we get from giving a gift is even greater than the
good feeling we have when we get one, because when
we give, we are acting more like God than when we
receive.

◈ If we want to become co-creators with God, we need
to act like God by sacrificing our needs for the needs
of others. This can add meaning and purpose to our
lives. If we act with kindness to our spouse, children,
parents, and neighbors, we are helping God provide
for His subjects. We become the "long arm of God,"
an extension of Him. Rather than transcending this
world and rising to the heavens, we bring God down
into this world to live among us.

◈ When we cultivate the seed of Godly potential that
God instilled in us when He "blew into Adam's nostrils
the soul of life" (Genesis 2:7), then we are achieving
our purpose: to grow into the best and most Godly
person we can become. This happens when we sacrifice
our needs to advance the well-being of others, since
we are acting like God by giving.

Chapter Twelve
Squeeze Play: Obligations

The score is tied in the late innings of the game. You have a runner on third base and you have to get him to score. The infield of the other team is playing in, in order to prevent a ball getting through to the outfield. The manager of the batting team calls for the most daring play in baseball — the squeeze play. On a signal from the base coach, as the pitcher winds up, the runner at third breaks for home, as if to steal home plate. The batter squares to bunt and he absolutely *must* make contact with the ball and bunt it in fair territory. Otherwise, the runner charging from third base will be thrown out by the catcher as a routine pitch arriving at home, since the catcher would need only tag the runner sliding into home plate. If the ball is bunted foul, the squeeze play cannot be tried again, because the element of surprise will have been lost. If executed precisely, the ball will be bunted toward the first or third baseline just as the runner slides into home. The runner will hopefully be safe and the run will score. It is truly the most exciting move in baseball because it is a "must win" situation. There are no second chances.

What are the elements that go into a successful squeeze play? The signal to call for the squeeze must be given by the base coach and understood by the batter and the runner. The runner must get a good jump on the ball as he charges for home. The batter must bunt, and the bunt must land in fair territory and at a perfect distance from home plate and not too close to the fielders — just halfway between home plate and the fielders. And it cannot be bunted toward the pitcher, just down either baseline. Everything must be perfect. There is no room for deviation.

In society we have tremendous respect for volunteerism. People voluntarily give of their time, money, and effort to work for a cause without remuneration. Volunteerism is also commendable in Judaism as an act of *chesed*, or kindness, as we described in the chapter "Hit and Run: Building a Community with Kindness." But there is something even more laudable than volunteerism and acts of *chesed*. And that is doing something because you are required to do it. The squeeze play is compared to the Jewish concept of performing a mitzvah as an act of obligation.

Mitzvah does not mean "good deed." It means "commandment." For example, giving one-tenth of your net income to charity is a mitzvah, a Torah obligation. It is not a good deed or a nice thing to do. You don't volunteer the charity; it is required of every Jew. The Talmud puts it this way: "Greater is the one who is commanded and performs the deed than one who is not commanded and who performs the deed" (*Kiddushin* 31a).

Why is it better to be commanded to do acts of kindness than volunteering to do them? The answer is that the Torah system of mitzvos, of performing the required 613 Torah commandments, is based on a sense of obligation to serve God. The Ten Commandments are not Ten Suggestions or Ten Nice Things to Do When There Is Nothing Exciting on TV. They are required by God not for His benefit, but for ours.

God gets no benefit from our performing the commandments. He is not happier, more uplifted, nor does He smile when we do them. God is perfect. He does not need anything — not even our fulfilling the mitzvos. He is not improved by our observing them and He is not unhappy when we fail to perform them. The commandments are not for God; they are for us. He has given them to us so that we can do His will and come closer to our own perfection and thereby achieve our destiny.

The 613 commandments are made up of 248 positive commandments and 365 negative ones. The positive commandments include believing in One God, keeping the Sabbath, honoring parents, observing the holidays, giving charity, and paying workers' wages on time. These are the "thou shalts" in the Torah. When we perform them, we build our spiritual selves and develop our soul's potential.

Some of the positive commandments help us develop our relationship with God, like letting the land of Israel lie fallow in the seventh year. This commandment reminds us that we do not own the land, that it is a gift from God. We thus maintain a sense of humility. We are not "self-made" men. This attitude helps build our character. It builds our soul.

Then there are 365 negative commandments, known as the "thou shalt nots," including do not murder, do not steal, do not commit adultery, do not embarrass your friend in public, do not gossip (even if it is true), and do not lie. When we refrain from violating these negative commandments, we keep our souls intact and prevent them from becoming tarnished or destroyed. Included in these 365 negative commandments are those that affect our relationships, like not being jealous of our neighbor, not hating our brother in our heart, not bearing a grudge, and not taking revenge. When we refrain from violating these commandments, we keep our relationships with others intact.

There are some negative commandments that deal with our relationship with God, including not cursing God, not believing in other gods, not eating food on Yom Kippur, and not eating bread on Passover. When we refrain from violating these commandments, we prevent the relationship with God from becoming eroded and distanced.

This system of 613 mitzvos was commanded by God, the Commander in Chief, symbolized by the Commissioner of Baseball in our baseball/Judaism model. Since these commandments are prerequisites to our fulfilling our personal and Jewish collective destiny, they are obligatory. It is not simply a good idea to perform them. We *have* to do them.

Imagine a wife saying the following to her husband: "You know, dear, marriage, with all its obligations and responsibilities, is so very demanding and difficult. Tell you what. You don't have to come home tonight. Why not take the night off? And when you do decide to come home, you don't need to talk to me. I know maintaining our relationship in the midst of your other obligations is just too tough."

If a wife said this you might suspect she was thinking of divorce. Why? Because if you make no demands and have no sense of commitment and responsibility, then it means you don't really care. It lends itself to a weak relationship. On the other hand, when both parties have a sense of obligation to the other — a sense of urgency and a focus on the needs of the other — then there is a bond of commitment. When one spouse makes demands on the other, it means that the demanding party wants and cares about the relationship. This spouse is demanding interaction and a give-and-take that strengthens and invigorates the relationship.

In studies on adultery, the main reason cited for infidelity is not passion. It is that the other person "needed me." When there are demands in a relationship, then the parties feel needed. When marriage makes demands on the partners, it means they respect each other. The underlying idea is that each person believes the other can help him. This creates trust that the other will be there for him. When I make demands on you, it means I respect the contribution you can make to our relationship.

In marriage, as in Judaism, we don't fulfill our obligations out of fear of what might happen if we mess up. We perform these acts of commitment because we want to connect with our spouse in marriage and strengthen our proactive relationship with God.

The word "mitzvah" comes from the word *tzav*, which means "connection." The mitzvos are avenues or pathways to connect with the will of God. God obligates us to fulfill the mitzvos because our raison d'être is to connect with our Source. That is how we can achieve our destiny. God does not want us to spend our lives seeking merely first-base physical pleasures when we can be hitting home runs and achieve our ultimate destiny by becoming as Godlike as possible. So He commands us to perform these mitzvos. But ultimately, we should want to perform them because they put us onto God's spiritual frequency. Through doing mitzvos we can come closer to knowing God and, in turn, ourselves.

Home Run Tips 🏏

In kabbalistic thought the word "mitzvah" means something even more than connection. It means "joining with" and "pairing." According to the mystical system of Kabbalah, when we do a mitzvah, God pairs with us. In other words, He comes into the world and joins us as we do the mitzvah. We do not rise into the heavens to join God; rather, doing mitzvos is the way we can bring God into the world — into *our* world. We have the power to bring spirituality into our lives by performing the commandments, which are not for God, but for us, to enable us to come closer to actualizing our potential — by developing our character and soul.

Chapter Thirteen

Of Managers, Base Coaches, and Umpires: Rabbis and Their Congregants

The managers of the baseball team lead the team by working on skills during team practice, setting team strategy, and calling special plays for the players to execute on the field. In Judaism, these are akin to the leading rabbis of the generation, known as *gedolim*, "those who are great in knowledge," who set public policy and guide those who observe the laws of Judaism.

There are many such *gedolim*, or great leaders, who reside in Israel, America, and Europe, who guide communities, lead the local community rabbis in inspiration, and decide important matters of Jewish law, known as "halachah," literally, "the way to walk." The local rabbis who lead a particular congregation are akin to the base coaches. They have daily contact with the players on the field — the members of the community — and they guide them in the daily practice of Judaism. Each community or synagogue appoints its own communal rabbi, which means "teacher."

The *gedolim* are not elected to their positions of leadership. They are recognized by the worldwide Jewish community by virtue of the breadth and depth of their knowledge of Jewish law and tradition. These are not official positions of authority; the *gedolim* are simply viewed as the *einei ha'eidah*, the "eyes of the community," as a result of their expertise in Jewish law and scholarship.

Even the greatest Jewish leader is known as a *talmid chacham*, a student of a wise person. Why isn't he called a "teacher"? He is called a "student" because even he is still learning and growing. Becoming a *talmid chacham*, a student of a wise person, is the highest aspiration in Jewish society. These *gedolim* can spend between eighteen and twenty hours a day steeped in study and in answering questions of Jewish law from their congregants and Jewish communities around the world.

In baseball, the "men in blue," the umpires, call the balls and strikes at home plate, call runners "safe" or "out" during plays at the bases, and keep order on the field. They are empowered by the Commissioner of Baseball to act as the on-field enforcers of the rules of the game. Do the *gedolim*, the leading rabbis of the generation, enforce Jewish law? No, they determine the applications of Jewish law and help guide individuals and communities in their personal and collective relationship with God.

This is the uniqueness of Judaism. The *gedolim* and the local rabbis know more Jewish law and Jewish philosophy than the average "player," the ordinary Jewish person who is a member of a community or synagogue. The more a person knows through the study of the Torah, the Talmud, and Jewish law, the more that person integrates into his mind a Godly intellect, known as *sechel Eloki*. Wisdom and observance make them Godly. But any Jew can become a scholar, and every Jew is expected to study the Torah, the Talmud, Jewish thought, and ethics every day. This means that any Jew can become a leader of the Jewish people, if he sets his mind to in-depth and long-term study of Torah.

We are expected to learn in classes with our *gedolim* and rabbis, but ultimately, the highest level of achievement is when two ordinary members of the community pair up and study daily on their own in a study partnership called a *"chavrusa."* In this sense, Judaism is self-monitoring and decentralized. Each of us is encouraged to become as learned and observant as we can in order to develop and strengthen our personal relationship with God.

As we said in the chapter "A Stand-Up Double: Love," on a scale of 1 to 10, if one party in a relationship loves and interacts with the other party with the intensity of 10, and the other party loves and interacts with the other with the intensity of 3, the overall strength of the relationship will be 3. The relationship is only as strong as its weakest link. In our relationship with God, He always gives 10. He is always there for us. But, He has given us free will, and that includes free will to choose how intense we want the relationship with Him to be. If we choose 9, then the relationship will be as close as 9. And if we choose to have a weak or distant relationship with God, then the relationship will be valued at 3. The choice is ours.

Each Jew is encouraged to seek guidance in matters of Jewish law and practice from his or her local rabbi or from one of the *gedolim*, as the *Ethics of the Fathers* states: "Choose for yourself a teacher" (1:6). This is an important message from which we can all learn. Even though we must acquire a sense of independence and personal responsibility by making our own decisions in life, we must make informed decisions. In order to do so, we have to admit that we are sometimes influenced by personal bias or desires, and our decisions are not fully objective, even though we profess that they are. This is where humility comes in again. We need to admit that we are sometimes too close to a situation to make an objective decision. That is why it is helpful for everyone to appoint for himself a rebbe — a personal rabbinical guide — with whom to discuss and review important issues and life decisions.

Home Run Tips 🏏

In effect, every Jew monitors his or her own relationship with God. In Judaism, there is no confession to a priest where you ask for forgiveness. Each person has a direct hotline to God and opens his or her heart directly in a personal dialogue with God, through prayer.

In addition to prayer, we can relate to God by studying His mind and will, which He revealed to us in the Torah. It makes sense that the Creator, who has a plan for the universe and everyone in it, would not have left us in the dark about how to fulfill the plan and our own destiny. He did this by revealing to us the Torah on Mount Sinai, which all of the world's monotheistic religions acknowledge as a fact of history. The Torah is accessible to anyone who wishes to put in the effort to study and learn. It does not belong to the elite or to the rabbis. It belongs to every Jew who wishes to study the 613 commandments. It belongs to every non-Jew who wishes to study the seven Noachian laws and their sublaws. Today, the Torah and its commentaries have been extensively translated and elucidated to provide everyone access to its wisdom. Even the Talmud, which is the elucidation and explanation of the five books of the written Torah, has been extensively and beautifully explained in English and is available at your local Jewish bookstore. Imagine opening the Talmud and entering into a dialogue with the great minds of Jewish history — Rabbi Akiva, Maimonides, Rashi. The study of Talmud turns us into time travelers as we go back in history to discuss Judaism with our ancestors.

Chapter Fourteen
Errors in the Field: Fire and Brimstone, Thunderbolts and Lightning

When a fielder makes a throwing error or when he fails to make a play that he "should have been able to make," he is charged with an error. Any run that scores due to the error is called an "unearned run" and does not figure in the pitcher's "earned run average." Does the manager yell at the player who makes an error? No. The fans may be disappointed, but they, too, understand that players are human and sometimes have lapses in concentration and make a mistake. There is no fire and brimstone, no sin. A little disappointment, maybe, but no yelling and screaming. It was just a mistake.

God understands that we sometimes fall short in performing the commandments. The error is called a *chet*, which does not mean "sin." The traditional translation of *chet* as "sin" is found in the King James version of the Bible. It is not a Jewish translation. The word *chet* in the Torah comes from the word *l'hachti*, which means "to miss the mark." It is akin to shooting a bow and arrow in archery and missing the target. When we do God's will by performing the commandments, then we are "on the mark"; we get closer to God, and our relationship with God is strengthened. By performing the commandments, we place ourselves into God's spiritual frequency. We become "like-minded" and therefore more Godlike. In contrast, when we fail to perform a positive commandment or violate a negative one, we miss the mark — in other words, we are distanced from God and fall short of achieving our destiny, which is to become as Godlike as we can be.

Calling this error a "sin" is thus incorrect. The word "sin" connotes fire and brimstone, thunderbolts and lightning, and great booming voices shouting "Sinner!" This is not the true definition of *chet*. It means we are far from God; there is a distance between our will and His will. We can close up that distance from God by doing *teshuvah*, "returning" to the path of God's will by correcting our negative deed or doing today what we should have done yesterday. *Teshuvah* gets us back on track and puts us in sync with God's mind.

In the Jewish system of spirituality, rectifying a mistake is not called "repentance." Repentance suggests that I have tarnished my soul and it needs to be repaired. In reality, the soul is always pure and can never be tarnished or damaged. My mistake will have created a blockage or a layer over the soul which has blocked my direct connection with God. So when I repair the mistake it is called *teshuvah*, meaning "returning" or "getting back on track." The *teshuvah* removes the layer blocking my relationship with God. We can now restore and regain our direct relationship. The distance has been bridged.

It is the same thing with human relationships. When we wrong or hurt someone, they may be apt to sever the relationship with us because we have broken their trust. They can no longer rely on us. What would it take for us to regain the trust of the person we wronged? I suppose the injured party would want us to recognize and admit it, apologize sincerely, and not do it again. These are the three ingredients recognized by Maimonides as the three requirements for one to be forgiven by God for a mistake we have made. We must have remorse, we must admit it verbally, and we must not repeat the mistake.

We can now understand why this system of commandments is obligatory. Sure, it is nice to go above and beyond the call of duty. We can volunteer and do acts of *chesed*, kindness, and thus do more than the Torah requires. But the main thing is to do exactly what the Torah does require. Then we put ourselves on the same page as God.

I get it — you are having a problem with the "O" word: obligation. No one wants to be told what to do. That's exactly my point! When we are told what to do by a parent, teacher, or person in authority, some bell goes off in our gut, brain, or soul that says: No way! I will not do anyone else's bidding. I am my own man! And when we overcome that inner sense of resistance and do it anyway — because God requires it — then we have gained a greater sense of humility, which in turn makes us more Godlike.

Imagine that — when we do God's will, we become more Godlike by humbling ourselves. And humility is one of the attributes of God, in the sense that He is not so lofty as to overlook the needs of the unfortunate. For example, in the Saturday evening prayer at the end of Shabbos, we speak of God's humility in that "He performs justice for the orphan and widow and loves the stranger, to give him food and clothing" (Deuteronomy 10:18).

So, when the batter and runner in the squeeze play execute the play exactly as they were told and taught by their manager, they will be performing the will of the manager. And he, from the vantage point of the dugout, sees the big picture of what the team needs. The runner must break for home at the right moment, the batter must bunt at the right moment and toward the right place. Then the run will score and the team will benefit. It is not a case of doing a voluntary act. There is no room for creativity. They must perform the command of the manager. Nothing else will do.

What about creativity? If we are commanded to perform the will of the manager so precisely, then where does the player's individuality come into play? It manifests not in the dry execution of the play, but in the passion and energy of the player.

Let me illustrate with a story I heard from one of my teachers in Jerusalem. Every night he would study and prepare his lectures in his home library while his neighbor, a member of the Jerusalem Symphony, would practice a new piece. That month it happened to be Mozart's Fifth, and the musician had invited my teacher to attend the opening-night performance, when world-class virtuoso Yitzchak Perlman would be the guest soloist.

After attending the performance, my teacher approached his neighbor and asked why the soloist's rendering of Mozart's Fifth sounded so different from what he had heard his neighbor practice during the last month. The musician said he would answer that question in one month's time, when another senior violinist, Yehudi Menuhin, would come to Jerusalem as the soloist for another performance of Mozart's Fifth. He invited my teacher to attend that performance as well.

After that second performance, my teacher understood. He heard Yehudi Menuhin play the same piece played by Yitzchak Perlman — and it, too, sounded different! The musician explained to my teacher that each soloist puts his own energy, passion, and interpretation into the notes and musical score. Neither Yitzchak Perlman, Yehudi Menuhin, nor my teacher's neighbor would dare change even one note of Mozart's Fifth — otherwise it would no longer be Mozart. What changed was their individual creativity while playing exactly the same notes. So, too, with baseball and Judaism. All players hit, run, and field, but their passion and hustle is unique to them.

Would we ever dream of changing God's law to be more up-to-date or modern? Does God's law ever get old? Is it like a container of yogurt with a sell-by date? No. The Torah system is as relevant and applicable today as it was thirty-three hundred years ago when it was given on Mount Sinai. As time goes on and science advances us into nanotechnology, we still face the same issues that faced Adam and Eve — morality, character development, and personal fulfillment. Progress has changed the way we conduct business, but it hasn't changed man's moral fiber or the way he conducts interpersonal relationships. That is what the Torah provides. The Torah is the musical score for interpersonal relationships and achieving our personal destiny. We all play the same Torah notes, but with our own unique expression and passion.

Home Run Tips

🏏 The rules of baseball are the same for everyone, and so are the fundamentals of the game. In Judaism, we all follow the same Torah commandments, but our personal experience, background, and energy is unique to us. Each person injects his unique personality and character into prayer. We all pray the same prayers — we would not change a letter — but our thoughts and interpretation are different. We all keep the same laws of Shabbos, but the flavor and tone of the songs and the warmth and energy at the Shabbos table differ from family to family. Each of us chooses a charitable or community project that makes us feel fulfilled. Therein lies our creativity and uniqueness in performance of these time-honored commandments.

🏏 Judaism emphasizes the individual's personal relationship with God. We do not believe in intermediaries. We do not even buy retail. We go directly to the manufacturer. So each Jews prays directly to God and relates directly to Him by studying the Torah, which is an expression of His "mind" and will.

We speak to God through prayer, and God speaks to man through the Torah. This is an ongoing, dynamic, personal relationship. The real engine of Jewish growth is through increasing our Jewish knowledge.

● Having two Jews discussing and arguing over the meaning of a Torah text or the Talmud is the ultimate spiritual experience. One can ask a rabbi for assistance in understanding a particular text, and we are encouraged to ask rabbis halachic (Jewish law) questions, but Jewish life is driven by the work of individuals, who are encouraged and guided by a rabbi — which means "teacher."

Chapter Fifteen
The Batting Slump: Dealing with Life's Challenges

During the grueling baseball schedule, which includes 162 games and spans six months, it often happens that even the best players get into a hitting slump. They have trouble concentrating, or something gets in the way of their swing, and they could go hitless or get only a few hits out of forty or fifty at bats. This is called a "batting slump," and it is bound to happen.

How does Judaism look at a personal slump, when life does not really go your way and you experience challenges which seem to get you down and sap your energy?

Judaism calls this a *nisayon*, a test. God is testing you because He wants you to grow. This is one of the hardest concepts to handle in life and causes many people to get angry with God and stop observing their faith. They cannot accept why "God would do this to them."

This feeling is certainly understandable. Why would a good God allow a child to die, or someone to lose his job or become ill? Why would a good person be put through pain and suffering? It seems unfair. And many people lose their faith in the face of such seemingly unfair treatment by God.

If we operate our lives on the premise that the purpose of life is to have pleasure, then, when we suffer, we are liable to conclude that we are failing to achieve the purpose of life — and we are apt to walk away from God.

The truth is that God does everything out of love. So when God challenges us, He is actually showing us great love by pushing us to achieve our life's purpose. Sure, the test hurts; it is meant to stretch us. Ask Michael Phelps. I don't suppose he found it fun to work out six hours a day in the pool for four years as he trained for the Olympics. But the painful and rigorous training stretched him to become the most successful Olympic swimmer in history, with eight gold medals in a single Olympics. Does he regret the pain of training?

When we are presented with difficulties, our faith in God is challenged and our faith in ourselves takes a hit. Our job at these times is to ask ourselves what inner strengths and resources we possess, based on our Baseball of Strengths outlined in the chapter "Getting on Base: Believe in God Because He Believes in You," and see how we can activate these personal resources and draw upon them to solve, or at least deal with, the challenge.

If we can solve the challenge, in other words, hit the curveball that God has pitched, then it is clear that the challenge was a test from God that was meant to bring out a dormant attribute in ourselves which will make us a stronger, nobler person. If the problem is insoluble, but is chronic and ongoing, it is clear that the challenge is not a test to be solved at all. Rather, it is a challenge to be coped with and endured in order to rectify our soul in some way. This is called *tikkun hanefesh*, which brings us to the concept of reincarnation.

The soul can return to this world a number of times in order to rectify an outstanding weakness or attribute, in other words, to complete unfinished business from a person's last incarnation in a previous lifetime. This is a kabbalistic concept, the analysis of which is beyond the scope of this work.

I will touch on one area of reincarnation, though, and that is to try to understand the tragic death of a child or young person, which is the hardest challenge for us to come to grips with and accept. Twenty years ago, my brother-in-law, my wife's brother, died in a car accident at the age of twenty while he was away from home studying in a yeshivah. When someone dies young, the kabbalistic understanding is that the person's soul, which existed in a previous incarnation, had only a small amount of spiritual work to accomplish in the present incarnation in order to fulfill its ultimate destiny. So if someone dies young, it is clear that the soul has completed its mission in this world. The soul then returns to a spiritual place called the "world of souls" (which is a part of the Garden of Eden) to await the arrival of the Messiah, at which time all souls will experience the resurrection of the dead. This resurrection is not a spiritual one alone; it is with body and soul (Rabbi Moshe Chaim Luzzatto, *Derech Hashem* 1:3:13).

How do we approach the sadness, the pain, and the "down" we inevitably experience when we are going through a challenge or slump? What happens when a plane loses power or an engine fails? Does the pilot give up and crash land? No. He coasts. He tries to go into glide mode and guide the plane until the motor reignites or until he can bring the plane to a coasting stop. So, too, with challenges. We can purposely put ourselves into coast mode when going through a challenge, realizing that we are expected to glide now.

In our spiritual lives we can sometimes (also known as often) experience a spiritual slump. We don't feel like praying, giving charity, or acting nicely to others. Why would God do that to us? Doesn't He want us to be spiritual? Yes. The issue is: What is the definition of spiritual? If it means being a servant of God, then I might as well give up now, because I can count on the fingers of one hand the times I actually achieved the level of being a servant of God. But the reality is that if you think you have "made it" as a servant of God, then you have lost it. The real definition of "spiritual" is someone who is *striving* to be a servant of God. That is why God causes us to go into batting slumps — because He wants us to regain the desire to be His servant purely out of free will rather than from a position of contentment or an easy life.

This explosion-implosion mode is an inherent part of the Torah system. God created the world with this system, as the Torah states: "And there was evening and there was morning, one day" (Genesis 1:6). Why didn't God start the day with the dawn? Why does every Jewish day and, of course, every Sabbath and holiday, begin at sundown? Why not start the day at 12:01 a.m. like the rest of the world? Why do we always have to be different?

God is teaching us something about the nature of life and of ourselves through this system. First there must be evening, which symbolizes crisis, ordeal, and challenge. Then, after we work through the ordeal and grow from it, we arrive at the dawn, the morning, and the clarity of a new sense of self. God integrated this idea in nature. And whatever happens in the world of nature is certainly not "natural." Rather, it is there for a reason — to teach us something about life and our destiny. That is the meaning of the word "Torah" — it means "instructions for living."

Home Run Tips 人

❧ There are times in life we call *hispashtus*, which are times of exuberance, enthusiasm, and expansiveness. When we are in a down state, it is called *tzimzum* (contraction), times of reflection and taking stock. Both of these times are part of the cycle of living. Flowers close up at night — and we look inward during times of challenge. When the sun comes up, the flower opens up. We can purposely put ourselves into coast mode, or *tzimzum* mode, when going through a challenge, realizing that we are expected to glide now.

If the purpose of life is not pleasure but the achievement of meaning and personal growth, then challenges can actually help us achieve our life purpose. Our job is to figure out how we can grow in character and values as a result of the slump and find more meaning in our lives as a result. We can then be an even better player when we come out of the slump.

Chapter Sixteen

The Commissioner of Baseball: God

The commissioner of baseball is in charge of the baseball universe. He represents the entire league and looks after the best interests of the teams in general and each player in particular. He negotiates the television and advertising contracts for Major League Baseball to ensure the livelihood of each team. He negotiates the collective bargaining agreement with the players' union and is the protector and overseer of league rules and salary caps. He guides baseball owners and serves the best interests of the fans. In short, he is involved, day and night, in preserving the integrity of the game.

God is in charge of the universe. He governs the world with a form of divine guidance called *hashgachah klalis*, which means that He maintains the ecosystem and the symbiosis between the rock, plant, animal, and human species. He makes sure the world continues toward its destiny. And He also guides those who enter into a relationship with Him with *hashgachah pratis*, personal divine guidance. He ensures that every individual has what he or she needs in order to achieve his destiny. He metes out fines for infractions of rules in order to keep people driving safely through life. He conducts random drug testing by sending us challenges to maintain our personal standards of behavior. He is interested only in giving to and not taking from the members of the universe. He runs the Hall of Fame, known as the World to Come, where every player is remembered for his contribution to the game of life.

The only difference between the commissioner of baseball and God is that God gets no salary, since He has no needs. God is perfect and lacks nothing. He gains nothing from running the universe. He is completely a giver — He gives because that is His nature. (The Commissioner of Baseball does have personal needs and he is not perfect. Sorry, Bud.)

But how do you enter into a relationship with a God you cannot see? You can experience His presence. When you fly a kite to a height of a thousand feet, you can barely see the kite. So how do you know it is there? Because you can feel the tug on the string. So, too, with God. If your soul is open to it, you can feel the tug of His presence. God hides Himself from direct view so as to allow us the free choice to decide whether or not we want to find Him or believe in Him. If He manifested Himself, we would have no choice but to believe in Him. Our task is to cut through the curtain that seems to hide God from view. We do this by seeking His hand in our lives. In this way we can get ever closer to Him. But there must be a search. And the search is a developmental process that takes time.

God's purpose in creating the universe is to allow finite human beings to relate to Him and thereby connect with and experience a taste of eternity. God Himself is unknowable; His essence is beyond human comprehension. He is beyond space and time. Since we live within space and time, we do not have the mental tools to understand His essence. The only thing that we do know about God is what He has revealed to us about Himself. He did give us a glimpse of His attributes (which is not the same thing as knowing His essence) when He forgave the Jewish people for their mistake of worshipping the golden calf. At that time, God told Moses the formula for attaining God's forgiveness: emulate God's Thirteen Attributes. God said: Act like Me, and you will be forgiven.

God's Thirteen Attributes are: *"Hashem, Hashem, Keil, rachum, v'chanun, erech apa'im, rav chesed, v'emes, notzeir chesed la'alafim, noseh avon, vafesha, v'chata'a, v'nakei* — God, God, mighty, compassionate, gracious, patient, kind, true, Creator of kindnesses for thousands of generations, forgiving, and pure" (Exodus 34:6–7). (I am purposely translating and will discuss only ten of God's Thirteen Attributes, since three of them are subsumed in the others and are too subtle to distinguish in the English language.)

In our lifelong journey of trying to find ourselves, we backpack, introspect, take tai chi, go for therapy, and attend courses in self-awareness, anger management, parenting, and time management. Life is one long process of self-discovery toward an understanding of our inner selves and the stuff of which we are made.

When we get to know God, we get to know ourselves. This means that we must define, as best as we can, God's attributes and then try to identify which of them He instilled in each of us. In other words, which one or two of these Godly attributes is your predominant attribute? Which one or two of these attributes is your driving force, the theme of your life? These are the attributes that describe the real you, because your true identity is found in the attributes of God that come most naturally to you.

It makes perfect sense: Since God is the ultimate independent reality, and He created us, then we need to identify in what way we are like God. God is totally independent of this world. We are dependent upon Him for life. God is the Source of reality. We exist within reality. So that part of ourselves which acts, tastes, and behaves like God is the most real part of ourselves.

It is closest to reality because it is that part of ourselves which is closest to and resembles its Source.

God's attributes are meant for us to emulate. By God's attributes, we mean the way He interacts with the world. They are the source of how we interact with the world. These are the attributes that reflect your *tzelem Elokim*, your divine potential.

Now let's identify which attributes describe your unique personality:

God, God: When God referred to Himself as "God, God," He was teaching us that He is the same God before we make a mistake that He is after we make a mistake. He does not change because of man's mistakes. He loves us just as much before and after we transgress His commandments. This means that God is consistent. He doesn't change His view of us. When we bring this Godly attribute into our own world, it translates into the human attribute of perseverance and consistency. This describes a person who drives forward and does not give up. It is a person who does not stop until the job is done. Is that your strongest attribute? Is this the overriding theme of your life?

Mighty: God is all-powerful. He is the Almighty. He can do anything He wants. He makes sandwiches and He makes mountains. He is the ultimate Source of independence and autonomy. He has so much power that He overcomes His own inner resistance to mercy. He wants the world to be run with ultimate justice, but He overrides His own will and tempers justice with mercy. As it says, "His mercies conquer His anger" (Talmud Tractate *Berachos* 7a). In human terms, this attribute is expressed on two levels: It is reflected in a person who is strong-willed, ambitious, and driven to succeed. This is leadership. It is a person with vision and aspirations. This is a person with power. On the second level, it is reflected in a person who also exerts power over himself — he has self-control and self-discipline. As it says in the *Ethics of the Fathers* (4:1), "Who is strong? He who subdues his personal inclination." He tempers his need for being right with the attribute of compassion. That is true might. Do these traits describe you?

Compassionate: God is benevolent. He has mercy on His creations. He loves us and shows us His love by giving us life itself. He is a Giver. In human terms, when we act with compassion and mercy toward others, we are bringing God's attribute of compassion into the world. Are you a compassionate, caring soul? Is that your essence?

Gracious: The Hebrew word for graciousness is *chein*. The American idea of graciousness is expressed in the all-American smile. However, smiles can be deceiving. Behind the cover of a "good morning" smile when you arrive at work, you can also be thinking, "I hate you, boss." Smiles can lie. I guess that's what it means when we say that a person is lying through his teeth. But a person's eyes don't lie. Real graciousness can be seen in the warmth and gentleness of someone's eyes. It is an empathic person who joins with another through sensitivity, sincerity, and humility. Graciousness is shown by the person who possesses a gentle, humble soul, expressed in the warmth of his eyes. Is empathy and graciousness the core of your personality?

Patient: God is patient. He waits for us to rectify and improve our behavior — to get our act together. In human terms, this is reflected in a person who is patient and laid back. When we act with patience toward others, we are bringing God's patience into the world. Is patience the strong point of your personality?

Abundant in kindness: God exhibits constant kindness. He provides for our every need, by granting us life, by sustaining our eyesight and hearing, and by healing our bruises. Are you a person who is always looking for ways to be helpful to others? Cooking meals for others when someone in the family is ill? Helping with community work? Visiting people in the hospital? This describes a giving, selfless person. Do you live to give?

Truth: Truth is God's signature. He runs the world with perfect justice that is balanced with kindness. If we step out of line even once, He should say, as did medieval rulers: "Off with his head!" But He doesn't. In human terms, when we act with honesty and integrity, we are bringing God's truth into the world. A person who always strives to do the right thing is driven by a sense of integrity. Is being careful not to hurt the feelings of others your modus operandi? Do you refrain from gossip and *lashon hara*, harmful speech? Do you return the extra change to the store? If so, you are a person who is driven by integrity.

Creator of kindness for thousands of generations: God is the Creator, and He has given some of us the power of creative energy. Are you a person who has creative ideas or is involved with creative projects? Do you play music or paint? Do you write? Are you a creative cook? When we use creativity, we are bringing the energy of God's creativity into our world.

Forgiving: God forgives. He gives us a chance to correct our mistakes. Are you a person who lets go of resentments, pain, and insults and gets on with life? If so, you are acting like God.

Pure: God created the world in general and you and me in particular for a specific reason. It is also pure, in the sense that it is perfectly suited to meet your soul's needs. He gave each of us a mission in life that only we can do. What is your unique reason for being in this world? In order to discover what this is, you need to find out what issue really moves and drives you. What is the theme of your life?

I know what you're thinking. *My mission? My life purpose? How do I know? That is too big a question for me.* It really isn't. The reason it feels like "too big a question" is because you probably haven't set your mind to it fully. You need to spend some time thinking about your strengths and positive attributes by taking a personal inventory of your personality strengths with the Baseball of Strengths that we outlined above. Once you have evaluated your strengths, then you can begin to figure out what God wants from you and what your life mission is.

Again, I know what you're thinking: *If I write down my positive strengths, it seems haughty and conceited.* I know it feels that way, but in reality it isn't. Conceit is past-oriented. It says, "Look at what I have accomplished. Look at what I have achieved. I deserve recognition and honor. Yes, that *is* conceit. But taking a personal inventory of the attributes and strengths that God has given you is not haughtiness; it is actually an act of humility — because it is future oriented. It says, "Here are the personal attributes and strengths that God has given me with which to serve Him. How can I use these strengths in the future to be a better servant of God? To quote my father, *z"l:* "How can I use these talents to help make this world a better place than when I entered it?"

The way to make this world a better place is to act like God. The Talmud (Tractate *Shabbos* 133a) explains the words of the song that the Israelites sang when they crossed the sea at the Exodus: "This is my God and I will glorify Him" (Exodus 15:2). How can I, a creature of flesh and blood, glorify God? By acting and being like Him, as the Talmud explains: As God is merciful, so, too, you must act mercifully. As God is gracious, so, too, you must act graciously.

The great Torah commentator Rashi comments that the Hebrew word for "glorify Him," *v'anveihu,* is made up of two words: *ani* and *Hu,* which mean "me" and "Him," namely, me and God. How do I glorify God? By being like Him. When I act Godlike I am glorifying God. I am bringing more of God's values and presence into the world. And by emulating God's attributes, I get close to God.

To become Godlike, we must act Godlike. If we use our free will to act like God, then we are accessing our positive inclination, our *yetzer tov,* which is the secret to victory over the negative inclination, the *yetzer hara.* When we access our Godly self through activating our positive inclination, we allow our positive or real self to be manifested. This transforms our very identity by activating our soul. By activating our Godly self, we bring more Godliness into the world.

Home Run Tips 🏃

꙳ When we act like God, we are achieving our life purpose, which is to be the best person we can become. In this way we are honoring God by bringing Him and His values into the world. And the only way to do that is to become as Godlike as possible.

꙳ Each of us is here in this world at this time because God has chosen us for a handpicked mission. Each of us has a job to do, and based on a review and analysis of the talents and values on our Baseball of Strengths, we can get a handle on what our life mission is, since it is related to our abilities. The attributes of God we have just reviewed in this chapter should be inserted in the section called "Personality" in your Baseball of Strengths.

This is the key to the personal strengths inventory that is the Baseball of Strengths. One of our life goals is to work on ourselves and to discover what our resources and abilities are and how we can use them to make a contribution to others and to society. This process of self-discovery is actually part of the process of becoming a servant of God. You serve God by using the talents and values He has instilled in you and use them to further His plan, goals, and standards. When you achieve self-discovery, then you put yourself in a position to actualize your potential. When you become the best person you can be, then you are achieving self-actualization, which simultaneously makes you into a servant of God.

Use the Baseball of Strengths as a system for self-discovery. Photocopy it and put it on your fridge. When you become aware of a new personal strength, then add it to your Baseball of Strengths. Whenever you are faced with a challenge, refer to your Baseball of Strengths and analyze which personal resources you can draw upon to deal with the challenge. Take the attitude that "I can handle this curveball. I have the talents and resources to meet this challenge. All I have to do is take the bat, which means: be aware of my strengths and step up to the challenge with confidence." This is called "Stepping up to the plate."

Chapter Seventeen
Stealing a Base: Turning a Liability into an Asset

The runner at first base takes a lead and inches his way further and further toward second base. The pitcher eyes him carefully using peripheral vision and waits before he winds up to see if he can make a throw to first base to catch the runner off the base. When the pitcher starts his windup toward the batter, the runner takes off toward second base with a fast jump in an attempt to steal second. The catcher receives the pitch and throws a line drive to the second baseman in an attempt to throw out the runner. He slides, and he's...safe! A stolen base.

The stolen base is perfectly legal in baseball, even though it is clearly a theft. The runner wants to advance into a position where he can score more easily on a hit. The pitcher, catcher, and second baseman work together to attempt to prevent the runner from stealing the base. From the point of view of the team in the field, the stolen base is a liability. From the runner's perspective, stealing a base is an asset. The runner wants to turn the defensive team's liability into an asset for his team.

In Judaism, when can we turn a liability into an asset? When you have a negative trait, and you channel it into something positive, then you are turning a liability into an asset. Such is the case with the three main negative human character traits: jealousy, desire, and honor

The *Ethics of the Fathers* states: "Jealousy, desire, and honor remove a person from the world" (4: 28). But how can it be that these traits are considered negative aspects of character? Didn't God Himself create human beings with these traits? The answer is that God placed these traits into man in order for us to learn to channel and transform them into positives. Every attribute that man has can be used for good. Each one must be innately positive, as it emanates from God. We, with our earthly frailties and flaws, distort and hijack these traits for our own purposes. Our challenge is to channel them by accessing our higher selves — our higher consciousness — and use these traits for positive purposes.

Jealousy can consume our energies. We can covet our neighbor's car, home, and lifestyle and ask, Why can't I have what my neighbor has? Much of our economy is driven by "keeping up with the Joneses." What we don't realize is that the Joneses' Lexus is what they need to fulfill their destiny, and our beat-up '87 Chevy van is what we need to fulfill our destiny. Perhaps we need to grow in character by increasing our humility and learning to live with less. If we could just focus on our own destiny and stop being distracted by the destiny of others, we would be on a faster track to our own fulfillment.

If all values are from God and therefore innately good, where is the goodness in jealousy? It can motivate me to become the best person I can become. If, as we said, knowledge and wisdom are among the highest values and acquiring them enables us to develop a Godly intellect, then we are entitled and even encouraged to be jealous of the knowledge and wisdom of others, as the Talmud says: "Jealousy of Torah study leads to increased wisdom" (Tractate *Bava Basra* 22a).

Thus, we are allowed to use our natural feelings of jealousy and channel them into being jealous of those who have greater Torah knowledge than we do. This will propel us to spend more time in study and will thereby increase our own wisdom. This is a valid use of jealousy. I am humbled by the fact that my neighbor has more wisdom than me, and that propels me to study more. This turns the liability of jealousy into an asset as it propels me to greater intellectual achievement.

What about desire? Desire has its origins, ultimately, in a yearning to be close to my Source, God. The reason God created desire is in order to increase our longing for a relationship with God. However, since we are made up of a Godly soul and an earthly body, our bodily needs hijack the purity of the desire for God and redirect it toward earthly passions. Our goal, or our test, is to channel the desire we experience and use it to grow as a person. In this way, we connect this human emotion of desire with the purpose of life — to become the best person we can become. We do this by attaching ourselves to God's standards of behavior and morality, which helps us get closer to God by improving our humanity and character. These standards are contained in the system of Judaism — which entails the performance of the Torah's commandments.

On the eve of Passover we are not allowed to have any matzah so that we will be able to eat the matzah at the Passover Seder that evening *b'tei'avon*, with desire. On the night we left Egypt we had no time to allow the dough to rise, so we ate matzah instead of bread. Thus, eating matzah on the night of Passover is a way to relive and reconnect with the spirituality of the Exodus. This is a valid and justifiable use of desire — to perform the mitzvah of eating matzah with desire and passionate interest in connecting with our roots. This is an example of how we can channel our desires to connect with God through the performance of the commandments.

Honor and pride come from a holy source — promoting the honor of God. When I have a natural inclination to promote my own ego and interests, I need, once again, to put this attribute into the context of achieving my purpose in life — to become the best person I can be. This means channeling my ego away from self-interest and toward humility. Whenever I feel pride in myself I can remember that the ultimate use of honor is to honor God. Thus, my purpose in life is to increase *kavod Shamayim* — the honor of Heaven — by making a *kiddush Hashem* — sanctifying God's Name. I can honor God by honoring His creations. When I give up my seat on a crowded bus to an elderly person, or let someone else in line ahead of me, or allow someone to cut ahead of me while driving from a side street — and smile as I do so — I am exercising humility and increasing God's honor.

Home Run Tips

🔸 When I experience a desire for something, I have to ask myself: Will acting on this feeling help me grow as a person? Will this choice I am a faced with make me more human or more animalistic? I need to put a "check and balance" on my feelings and channel them toward being Godly.

Chapter Eighteen
Fielder's Choice: Free Will

With a runner on first, the batter hits the ball to the shortstop. The shortstop doesn't have enough time to try for a double play, so he needs to decide whether to throw the ball to second to get the lead runner out or throw to first. He would rather get the lead runner out, but if the lead runner has a good jump on the ball, the shortstop may not want to risk getting no one out, so he may elect to throw to first to get the certain out. It is a matter of choice. It is called "the fielder's choice."

Judaism believes that the foundation of human existence is that God has given human beings free choice, or free will, with which to organize our lives. We have free will to choose a career path, where to live, whether or not to believe in God, or whether to have apple pie or watermelon for dessert. God does not control our decisions. If He did, then there would be no such thing as reward or punishment, since we would be like preprogrammed automatons.

It does not really matter whether we have apple pie or watermelon for dessert. It does not matter whether we remodel our kitchen in blue or green. These choices do not affect the balance of the universe. However, whether or not we choose to give charity or to lie or tell the truth *does* have an affect on the cosmos. Decisions we make in the area of good and evil, whether to help or hurt someone, or to cheat or act honestly, have an affect, not only on the recipients of our deeds and decisions, but on the quality of our own character.

Making the right moral choices is a matter of personal conscience. We need to be able to live with ourselves by making moral decisions that leave us feeling *shalem*, or whole, with our own inner selves. The world *shalom* means "peace," and when it is applied to ourselves it means that we strive for inner peace, or inner balance. If our inner equilibrium is not congruent with our moral values, then we may come to feel uneasy with our "selves" and experience emotional turmoil. We can hardly function with confidence in that state of mind.

There is a new sport called "ice waterfall climbing." The sportsman climbs up a two hundred-foot-high, frozen-over waterfall with mountain-climbing gear. Every step he takes is a life-and-death decision. One of these climbers was interviewed and asked why he risks his life like that. He answered: "In my everyday life, going to work, interacting with friends, going shopping, none of my decisions really counts. My life is dry and insignificant. But up on the waterfall, every move I make counts. I feel like my decisions up here matter. Up here, I feel alive."

The climber has created a contrived significance in his life. His decisions on the waterfall count only because he has forced the hand of destiny and put himself in a contrived situation of danger so that he can "feel" like his decisions count. In Judaism, every moral decision we make is significant. And whether to help someone, speak good or ill of another, or refrain from raising one's voice at one's spouse, does count and does affect the cosmos. This exercise of free will in the realm of moral choices, which are guided by Jewish law, makes every act we do signifi-cant. We are always alive.

The Torah says: "I have placed before you the good and the bad, life and death, so choose life" (Deuteronomy 30:19). God is rooting for us from the Commissioner's private box. He wants us to feel a sense of inner balance and conscience. He wants us to be able to live with ourselves, but He isn't going to force Himself on us. We must remember that we have been given the power, but not the authority, to choose. We must use the power of choice delicately and not forcefully. God will not force our hand and make us do the right thing; He doesn't want us to use our power of free will to force the hand of others, either. He wants us to choose to do it for ourselves and by ourselves, not for His benefit, but for our own growth in moral character. We can thus choose to be like God.

In addition to being a matter of conscience, it is also a mat-ter of objective truth. I know that it is not politically correct to suggest that there is one absolute truth; it does not sit well with the values of a liberal democracy. We like to suggest that everyone is entitled to his opinion. Everyone has a right to live his own life.

In America we all like to say that we are "one nation un-der God." We put God on our money and say: "In God We Trust." And as if that weren't enough, we perform the ultimate act of faith and spirituality: we sing "God Bless America" at ball games. Yes, we believe in God. But what are the ramifications of that belief? Is belief simply a matter of the heart? If one believes in God, then the next logical step is that we have obligations and responsibilities to perform in order to adhere to the stan-dards of behavior that are required by that God. And there are consequences for not following those standards.

My father used to love telling the following joke: Two par-ties to a dispute come before the rabbi and each tells his story. The rabbi turns to the first litigant and says, "You are right." Then the rabbi turns to the second litigant and says, "You are right."The rabbi's assistant asks the rabbi, "How can they both be right?" And the rabbi answers, "You are right, too!"

There can be only one right pathway when it comes to moral choices. Just because a country passes a law does not make it morally correct. The fact that the Dutch parliament has legalized assisted suicide is objectively wrong from God's moral standards. Says who? Says the Talmud and the *Code of Jewish Law*. Someone needs to take a stand and tell it like it is. God does.

Home Run Tips

- Our choices in the area of morality do make a difference, not only in the lives of others, but also in our own moral fiber.

Chapter Nineteen
Double Play: This World and the World to Come

With a runner on first, the batter hits a ground ball to the shortstop, who picks up the ball and flips it to the second baseman covering second base to get a force out at second. Then the second baseman fires the ball quickly to first base to get the out at first, and voila! A double play. Two outs in one swift play.

The double play of Judaism is the duality that God built into the universe. There are various "double plays":

1. *Night and day*
2. *Good and evil*
3. *The positive inclination and the negative inclination*
4. *The written Torah and the oral Torah*
5. *This world and the World to Come*

The written Torah consists of the Five Books of Moses, namely, Genesis, Exodus, Leviticus, Numbers, and Deuteronomy. God explained the meaning of the written Torah to Moses on Mount Sinai and through ongoing discussions with him in the Sinai Desert during the forty years the Israelites wandered there. These verbal explanations of the written Torah became known as the "oral Torah." The written Torah became the "lecture notes" to the ongoing oral dialogue between God and the Jewish people. This oral Torah was taught by Moses to the children of Israel, and they in turn passed it down to every succeeding generation until it was finally written down between 200 CE and 500 CE and became known as the Talmud. Scholars and lay people study the Talmud daily.

When God created the world, there was only one world — the Garden of Eden. Adam and Eve were created on a Friday, placed in the Garden of Eden, and given one commandment — to eat from all the trees in the garden except the tree of knowledge of good and evil. Had they succeeded in following that commandment, they would have entered into the Sabbath (which begins on Friday night at sundown) in perfect harmony with God's will, which would have brought the world to perfection. Perfection is achieved when man brings Godliness into the world through following God's will.

And where would we human beings have been had Adam and Eve brought the world to its perfection on that first Sabbath of the world's existence? We would have also been in the Garden of Eden, as "we" would have been contained in the souls of Adam and Eve. After all, we are their offspring. If they would have been in the Garden of Eden on the Sabbath, we would have been there, too. In them! Since they failed to follow God's will, God had to put them (and their future children — us) through a proving ground in order for them to earn their right to get back into the Garden of Eden. So He created a two-stage process. The Garden of Eden became the place of reward — the World to Come — and the world we know as the earth became the proving ground — this world.

How do we earn our reward in the World to Come? By performing the Torah's 613 commandments in this world. When we perform the Torah's commandments, we create a spiritual energy that we will reside in, and gain the benefit of, in the World to Come.

Why doesn't the written Torah itself refer to the World to Come? Why is it referred to only in the oral Torah? The answer is that Judaism is not based in the World to Come. Rather, it is based on this world. Our goal in this world is to delight in God by having a relationship with Him through living in accordance with His values and standards (Rabbi Moshe Chaim Luzzatto, *Mesillas Yesharim* [*The Path of the Just*]).

Some people have the misconception that we earn brownie points when we perform the commandments in this world and we cash them in when we get to the World to Come. They think that the World to Come is like a county fair where you cash in your tickets for worldly prizes like a Lexus, a Jacuzzi, a mansion, and vacations. This is not how it works.

In this world, when we follow God's will, we create a spiritual force field, and the force field is *itself* the World to Come. When we perform a mitzvah, we create a spiritual energy which we will "live in" and experience in the World to Come. When we perform the commandments, we effectively reunite this world and the World to Come, as they were originally one world. These two worlds were split when Adam and Eve made their tragic mistake and were banished from the original world, the Garden of Eden. The positive energy we create by performing commandments in this world effectively creates a bridge to the World to Come. It is this bridge that becomes our reward — forever, in the World to Come. The spiritual delight that we will experience in the World to Come, as a result of performing the commandments in this world, is currently beyond our ability to comprehend. It is the delight of dwelling in the divine presence forever. We can get a taste of that delight while in this world when we experience the Sabbath.

If there are two worlds, then why aren't they called *this* world and *that* world, as if they were two separate entities? The answer is that this world *gives birth to* the next world, via our free will actions. That is why the next world is called the World to Come...because it comes *out* of this world. Effectively, then, in the World to Come we will relive the spiritual energy we created in this world. That is why our actions in this world are so precisely measured and valued by God. That is why the written Torah does not mention the World to Come explicitly. God wants us to work on ourselves in this world and to perfect it. Our actions have cosmic and eternal significance, in this world. God must think a lot of us to give us so much responsibility.

Home Run Tips 🏃

◍ Live life the right way now, in this world.

Chapter Twenty

The Stadium, Game Time, and the Fans: Place, Time, and Soul

The radio announcer, the local voice of baseball, announces in dramatic fashion: "*Here we are, folks, at classic Bolton Stadium, home of our heroes, the Bolton Bombers, as we approach our 1:05 game time in this decisive game during this pennant race. And besides having a great and competitive team, we have, as we have had for the past eighty-five years, the best and most loyal fans in Major League Baseball...you, the Bolton Bomber fans!*"

A day at the ballpark is an all-American experience: The stadium; the national anthem; the vendors; the hot dogs; the spirit; fans streaming to the ballpark by bus, by car, by subway, and on foot; the anticipation as game time approaches that *maybe this will be our year*; the strains of "Take Me Out to the Ball Game."

In Jewish thought we can categorize three key baseball elements as the key elements of life:

Olam — the stadium, the physical world

Shanah — game time, the world of time

Nefesh — the fans, the world of people, souls

Any given moment can be characterized as having a physical dimension (the stadium), a time dimension (game time), and a people, or soul dimension (the fans). The stadium represents the physical location where the event, activity, or action takes place. We need to be aware of and appreciate our physical surroundings — the stadium, or setting, where the events of our lives unfold. In order to get the most out of life, we need to be conscious of where we are — at home, at work, or at play — and that awareness allows us to plug into the appropriate mode of behavior for that particular location.

Game time represents that mysterious facet of life called time. The verse in the Torah that says, "In the Beginning God created the Heaven and the earth" (Genesis 1:1) makes us aware that God created "the beginning"; He created time itself.

God Himself is beyond time. He is in the past, the present, and the future simultaneously. As created beings in God's world, we need to be aware of the passage of time and be plugged into the special moments of our lives. Otherwise, we will miss them — and with them, life itself will pass us by.

For God, time is infinite. For us, it is not. That is why we need to be aware that we have a limited time within which to achieve our personal destiny. We need to spend real time, not just "quality" time, with our kids and our spouse. We need to "be there" in the moment as we teach our kids to read, to play in the sandbox, to ride a bike, to do homework projects, how to have a conversation, how to relate to others, and how to make the right moral choices.

I was twelve years old and sitting in our car on a Sunday morning, getting ready to depart for a family outing to the beach in Long Sault, Ontario. I watched my seven-year-old sister (she is now forty-two) skip down the path from our house toward the car with her sand pail and blow-up toy in hand. At that moment I remember asking myself, "I wonder when life is going to start?" And at the same moment, I answered my own question: "Wait a second. Going to the beach with my family on a Sunday — it doesn't get any better than this. There is nothing else. This *is* life. It is happening here and now." That is when I started to become aware of time. At that moment, I began to appreciate the here and now and to live in the moment. That is when I started to become aware that I was alive.

The third dimension of life is the soul dimension, the fans, the people who are in my field of vision, in this stadium — in this place — at this time. These are the most important people in my life, with whom it is intended that I interact and with whom I am supposed to enter into a give-and-take relationship. The convergence of these three elements — people, place, and time — will never be duplicated. It is unique, and it is incumbent on me to get all I can out of this matrix. This is called being present and living consciously in the here and now.

I had a "convergence" moment when I was leading a tour of high school students on a summer experience in Israel last summer. Our group studied Torah in the mornings and toured and hiked the country in the afternoons. We took a ride to the Jordan Valley and entered rafts for a kayaking trip down the Jordan River.

I entered a kayak and followed the group along the narrow and gentle waters of the Jordan River, the same river the Jewish people crossed as they entered the land of Israel after they left Egypt. I saw the rocky banks of the river, the willow trees with their branches overhanging the river, the red dragonflies and brown- and blue-winged birds, and I was moved to sing the words of Psalms from the Hallel prayer (from the word *hallelukah*, which means "praise God") that we sing on Jewish holidays.

I was very moved by the experience. I felt close to God. It was a moment of awareness of my finite self connecting and relating to my infinite Source, a moment of spirituality. And just then I realized why. The world is divided into four categories, as we talked about in the chapter "A Triple: Integrity — the Challenge of Being a Good Person," and here I was experiencing them all, simultaneously:

Domem — inanimate objects: the banks of the Jordan River

Tzomei'ach — plant life: the overhanging trees and vines leaning into the Jordan

Chai — animal life: red dragonflies, brown- and blue-winged birds

Medaber — the speaker: man, me, praising God for connecting all of this nature to its Source through singing Hallel, praises to God from the Psalms.

Why is the fourth level in the system above called "the speaker" as opposed to "man"? The essence of something is its purpose. The purpose of man is "to speak" — to communicate and to connect the physical world with its Source. That is why the ultimate use of speech is prayer, and that is why prayer is a spiritual connection with the Source. In other words, as I was kayaking down the Jordan River, I captured a mini picture of life: soil, plants, animals, and me — the speaker — uplifting the finite scene by connecting it to its Source, God. In that moment I felt alive, because I was connecting and relating to the Source of life itself.

This physical space — the world — was the Jordan River. The time was the summer of 2009. The souls — me and my students. The convergence of these three elements never happened before in world history and will never happen again. If I am truly "awake" and appreciate this convergence, then I become truly alive in the moment. I can fix that moment in my consciousness and revisit and reexperience that convergence moment anytime I wish.

Home Run Tips 🏃

◈ When we go through the motions of life, we tend to function on autopilot.

◈ If we want to capture life's drama and truly "live," we need to "show up" by waking up out of our automaticity and into the mode of living consciously.

◈ Being aware of the physical place we are in, the time of day, and the people we are with at that moment is a framework to focus on so that we can live the moment fully.

◈ The convergence of place, time, and people never happened before in world history and never will again. Life is a series of these place, time, and people moments. Being conscious of these convergence moments will allow me to seize each moment and to truly get the most out of life.

Chapter Twenty-One

Fundamentals of the Game: Getting Back to Basics — the Sabbath, Keeping Kosher, and Family Purity

The key elements of baseball are hitting, fielding, and teamwork. Hitting is the offense, fielding is defense, and teamwork is ultimate cooperation. In Judaism, too, we can finds these three elements, which make up the fundamentals of Jewish life:

> *Offense* — observing the Sabbath
>
> *Defense* — keeping kosher
>
> *Teamwork* — following the laws of family purity

Observing the Sabbath is the positive act of connecting with God by recognizing that He is the Source of the creation and I am not. When we say that God created the world in six days, we mean that He put into play the laws and processes of the natural world, including gravity, electromagnetic forces, nitrate systems, reproductive systems, and laws of conservation of energy, to name but a few.

God put human beings into the world in order for them to use these natural systems to progress and to achieve world peace; to eradicate disease, poverty, and hunger; and to make this world a place where God would be happy to join us. We move the world toward these goals by showing our creative mastery over it through plowing, planting, reaping, shaping, pruning, burning, baking — in other words, by producing.

We are commanded by God to recognize on the Sabbath that God is the Source of creative energy and production in the world, and we are required on the Sabbath to rest from our creative mastery over the universe. That is why on the Sabbath Orthodox Jews don't turn the lights on and off, drive a car, plant or water seeds, or go to work: we stop the personal creative process and spend one day plugging into the Source of creativity — God. We thereby recognize that God is the Master Creator. This is called "keeping Shabbos." We keep, or observe Shabbos by having family meals, going to synagogue to pray, studying, engaging in self-reflection, and suspending our creative energies. Keeping Shabbos is like having a good offense in baseball. When a team has good hitters who get on base and drive in a lot of runs, they move the team toward success. Being a good spiritual hitter is achieved by keeping Shabbos, by being humble enough to know that you are not the source of your own creative power.

The observance of Shabbos is the most holistic and energizing use of our time. Imagine a twenty-five-hour period where you are not forced to run to answer the phone, do errands, or be a slave to work. When we observe Shabbos, we free ourselves from slavery to man-made technology and get back to basics. We leave the world in its original pristine state. We don't exploit or progress the world; we become at ease and at one with the universe.

Some psychologists suggest to their clients that they take

their families out of the city for a twenty-four-hour country experience where they leave the pressures of their daily routines and get back to basics — family bonding time, a walk in the woods, some quiet reflection. This is what Shabbos does, and we do it every week.

The seventh-inning stretch in baseball takes place halfway through the seventh inning. The game takes a short break where the fans stand up, stretch their legs, and sing, "Take Me Out to the Ball Game." It adds a little fun just before the last few innings of the game. Shabbos is like the seventh-inning stretch. We have been living the game of life intensely, and now it is time to take a spiritual break, reflect on the game of life, and sing a song at the Shabbos table. The seventh-inning stretch gives us a chance to review the events of the game of life so far and renew our energies.

Shabbos creates a rhythm of creativity and reflection that reconnects us with our inner selves. We get in touch with our Godly creativity by refraining from creative mastery over the world. When we plug into the Source of creativity, we recharge our spiritual selves and start to live again.

If you want to experience a real holistic Shabbos where you get to rediscover yourself, I would be happy to arrange for you to spend a Shabbos with a Shabbos-obsevant family in your community, anywhere in the world. I know a lot of people. Just e-mail me at thebaseballrabbi@aol.com

Having a good defense in baseball is symbolized by following the Jewish dietary laws — by keeping kosher. There are three categories of keeping kosher:

1. We eat meat or other animal products only from domesticated animals that have split hooves and chew their cud — like cows, sheep, and goats. We are also allowed fowl, which do not prey on other animals. We are allowed to eat fish that have fins and scales — and which do not prey on other fish. The reason for this

is that "you are what you eat," so we cannot eat foods from animals that trample or prey on other animals. We must learn to become people of domestication and gentleness rather than preying on others. We must learn to be "defensive," so to speak, rather than aggressive. That is what I call the dietary laws — the defensive laws, or the fundamentals of fielding, since they are designed to make us more defensive and docile rather than aggressive and hurtful.

2. We cannot eat the flesh of a cow, sheep, goat, or fowl unless it was slaughtered in the most humane way possible. It must die almost instantly via a perfectly sharp knife which cuts the jugular vein and the windpipe of the animal simultaneously, with a single forward motion. The animal does not suffer. It is like getting a paper cut — you don't realize you have a cut until a few moments later when the air hits the wound. By that time the animal has already died. The animal also cannot be shot, stunned, or drowned. It must be slaughtered in a manner where it suffers least, so as to develop our sense of "defensiveness" and sensitivity to creatures of God's world.

3. We cannot eat or cook meat and milk together. Meat represents the physical world of the flesh. Milk represents the nurturing of a mother nursing its young. These two concepts must not overlap. We must temper our physical desires with nurturing and kindness — we must learn to be defensive and gentle rather than taking the offensive.

The third fundamental of baseball is teamwork. The ultimate example of teamwork in life is the harmony and joint effort of the marriage relationship. The secret glue of that relationship is mutual respect and giving, which finds its ultimate expression in intimacy.

In accordance with Jewish law, when a woman has her period, plus an additional seven days (usually a total of twelve or thirteen days), a husband and wife refrain from any physical contact. After this physical separation, the woman has a spiritual reconnection with the waters of life, immersing in a *mikveh*, a beautiful ritual bath. On the twelfth or thirteenth night of this cycle, after immersing in a *mikveh*, she and her husband resume their intimate relationship. Imagine injecting this kind of renewal in a couple's marriage. A husband and wife treat each other like a bride and groom, every month. This system, which is built upon Judaism's laws of family purity, gives the couple a sense of teamwork in that they are working together to build a wholesome relationship where spirituality, communication, respect, and intimacy all have their place.

Home Run Tips 𝕏

The three fundamental principles of Jewish life are observing the Shabbos, keeping kosher, and adhering to the laws of family purity. Shabbos puts you in harmony with the world. You leave the world alone while you reflect on your place in the universe. Keeping kosher puts you in touch with yourself. It makes you conscious of what you eat and how we relate to the plant and animal world. It makes you contemplate who you are — the stuff you are made of — as we say, you are what you eat. The laws of family purity put you in harmony with your spouse. The laws create a rhythm of togetherness and then separation so that the overall relationship can be balanced with communication, respect, and giving — and they put that togetherness into that context. Intimacy is meant to build the overall bond between the spouses and is not seen as an end in and of itself.

Chapter Twenty-Two
Pitch and Catch

Probably the phrase most used by North American boys is: "Wanna pitch around?" In other words, "Do you want to play pitch and catch?" There is nothing more all-American, more bonding than when two friends throw a baseball back and forth in someone's backyard or in an open field. Wherever there is an unused swath of grass, you may well find two boys or a father and son playing pitch and catch. There is something poetic in the silent bond of the throw-and-catch rhythm. The sound of the ball hitting the pocket is the sound of success, the sound of "all is well with us." This is where baseball leaves the world of sports and enters the realm of the spiritual.

The pitch and catch of Judaism can be found in the question-and-answer method of Jewish study in the study hall. Enter a library at Harvard or Oxford and you will enter the rarefied world of scholarship, with students silently poring over their journals and tomes with the utmost concentration and focus. Now enter a Jewish study hall in any yeshivah, or place of learning, and you will experience the *milchemta shel Torah*, the war of Torah study. Each study partner is raising his voice to his learning partner sitting opposite him and arguing with him about the meaning of a particular passage of the Talmud. Imagine five hundred people all at the same time and in the same place arguing loudly with each other and demanding that the other understand his point and why he's got it wrong. And yet it is the most beautiful sound in the world, because it is the *kol Torah*, the sound of Torah. Why are students allowed to be strong-minded with their study partners and even become strident with each other? Because they are arguing about truth and how one should decide a particular point of Jewish law.

There is another type of pitch and catch that I experienced on a Shabbos visit to the house of my friend Zalman Nissel of Baltimore. I noticed amidst the elegant silver serving pieces in their dining-room breakfront a softball with writing on it. It was something like the children's game, "Which item doesn't belong in this picture?"

I asked Zalman what the ball was doing there. Zalman answered that he used to play pitch and catch with his learning partner, Yaakov, during lunch breaks at his yeshivah. They would toss the ball back and forth and talk about stuff and life and the future. They became very close friends. After many years of studying together, they both went on to college and got married. When Yaakov had his first child, Zalman attended the celebration, and when he spoke at the luncheon he presented Yaakov with the best possible gift — the baseball they used to throw back and forth — as a symbol of their friendship and closeness. On the baseball Zalman wrote: "Mazel tov on the birth of your daughter, Esther, June 1987."

A year later, Zalman's wife had a baby girl, and when Yaakov attended the celebration he spoke at the luncheon and presented Zalman with the very same baseball, this time with an added inscription: "Mazel tov on the birth of Devorah, September 1988." There are now twelve inscriptions on the baseball, and the learning partners send it back and forth to each other, sometimes in person and sometimes by FedEx, when each has a birth, bar mitzvah, or wedding, and now births of grandchildren. Such is the love that was found in the game of pitch and catch between two *chavrusas*, or learning partners, who became bound together in friendship as they argued with each other to discover the truth so many years before. Long may the pitch and catch continue.

Home Run Tips

The real joy of Jewish life is the relationship created when two learning partners study Torah together. Children can bridge the generation gap with their grandparents as they study the Torah and Talmud together. When two partners learn Torah together, the divine presence rests upon them, because they are studying something bigger than both of them. They are discovering God's will in a particular area of Jewish life and Jewish law. If you are interested in finding a study partner in your city, please e-mail me at thebaseballrabbi@aol.com, and I will set you up to study with someone on the topic of your choice.

Chapter Twenty-Three
The Relief Pitcher: Transmission to the Next Generation

The art of relief pitching is when the starting pitcher has taken his team into the middle innings of the game — hopefully the sixth or seventh inning — and begins to tire, whereupon the manager calls in one of his relief pitchers to take over the pitching duties and hopefully finish the game. The manager takes a slow walk to the pitcher's mound to allow the relief pitcher more time to warm up in the bull pen and then speaks to the starting pitcher on the mound. Then the dramatic moment arrives: the manager asks the pitcher to hand him the ball, the manager pats him on the shoulder, the crowd (usually) cheers, and the pitcher walks slowly off the mound to the dugout. The manager then hands the ball to the relief pitcher and he begins to warm up on the mound. It is a bittersweet moment. The pitcher has done his best, and now it is time to move on and hand the job over to someone with a more rested arm.

This moment of transition from starting pitcher to relief pitcher can be compared to the transmission of Torah knowledge, wisdom, and tradition from one generation to the next. Abraham lived for when he could transmit the values of belief in one God and moral behavior to his son Isaac. God was impressed that Abraham wanted those values to continue into the next generation and thus chose him as the father of the Jewish people. Abraham chose to believe in God as the Creator and Master of the universe, and so we became the "choosing people." God in turn chose Abraham, and we thus became the chosen people.

God chose the Jewish people for the mission of bringing the idea of One God to the world. Belief in One God brings with it a commitment to act in accordance with one universal standard of behavior — absolute morality. We have laws on abortion, euthanasia, and who gets a kidney transplant. It is a system that places morality into the context of laws commanded by God. That is why monotheism represented such a great advance and contributed to civilizing the world. And it was Abraham's willingness and desire to pass this belief system on to his son Isaac that impressed God, as He said, "To your children I shall give this land" (Genesis 15:18).

The transmission of Judaism's values to the next generation is called the transmission of the *mesorah*, or tradition. The opening statement of *Pirkei Avos*, or the *Ethics of the Fathers*, the classical compendium of ethical life skills and values, states, "Moses received the Torah from God at Mount Sinai and transmitted it to Joshua. Joshua transmitted it to the elders of Israel. The elders transmitted it to the prophets, the prophets to the Men of the Great Assembly" (1:1*)*.

The process of transferring and teaching the Jewish spiritual heritage to the next generation is one of the most significant ideas in Judaism. In modern terms we say, "Don't just keep the faith — pass it along!"

When we speak of Jewish values, we are not speaking merely of Jewish ideas and feelings. Rather, we are referring to the practical process of living in accordance with Jewish law. Many people today are not conversant with Jewish law, or they simply find the laws too onerous and therefore say, as I have heard many times, "I don't follow Jewish law, but, Rabbi, I feel Jewish in my heart. That's the most important thing." The truth is, feeling Jewish in your heart is not enough. Why not? Because we cannot transmit feelings from our heart to our children without a concrete system of law and tradition. The feelings of connection to Judaism and Jewish pride come from Jewish practice — observance of the Sabbath, keeping kosher, and observing the laws of family purity. These are the three pillars of Judaism. All the other laws are based on these fundamentals.

We call Jews who don't observe the laws of Judaism and feel Jewish only at heart and in spirit members of cardiac Jewry. It is not a fulfilled and meaningful Judaism, because it will not be continued in the acts and daily living of the children and grandchildren, which is the litmus test of Jewish continuity. We cannot transmit to the next generation a "feeling" of being Jewish or theoretical concepts of Jewish culture and Jewish values. Feelings and values cannot be transmitted to the next generation unless they are contained in tangible actions. When you concretize the values and feelings into the system of laws called mitzvos, then they can be conveyed to the next generation.

Let us take a look at some special transmission moments in the Jewish life cycle:

Circumcision: A circumcision, which is called a "bris," literally, "covenant," is a special ceremony that takes place when a baby boy is eight days old. A Jewish doctor or mohel (a person trained in carrying out this procedure according to Jewish law) surgically removes the baby's foreskin. This was commanded by God in the Torah, as it states, "On the eighth day you shall circumcise the foreskin" (Leviticus 12:3).

The ceremony is sealed with a blessing made by the father, who says: "Blessed art Thou, O Lord...who has commanded us to cause this child to enter into the covenant of Abraham, our father." The father, bringing his son into the covenant of Judaism, performs the first act of transmission. It initiates a process whereby the father gives and the child receives instruction in Jewish law and values. It is like the starting pitcher giving the ball over to the relief pitcher. The game will go on.

It is not a tradition or quaint legend or folklore to participate in the transmitting of Jewish values and laws to the next generation. Rather, it is a mitzvah, a Torah commandment, as the Torah states, "And you shall diligently teach your children" (Deuteronomy 6:7).

As the circumcision is performed and after the father makes his blessing (which never fails to send a bolt of spiritual lightning through my soul), all of the assembled guests respond out loud, "Just as he has entered into the covenant of Abraham, so may he enter into Torah, the marriage canopy, and the performance of good deeds." The transmission process thus begins when a baby is eight days old.

What is the significance of the mitzvah of circumcising the baby on the eighth day? The number 7 has many applications in Judaism. The Sabbath is on the seventh day, there are 7 weeks between Passover and Shavuos, the bride walks around the groom 7 times, there are 7 species of special fruits of the land of Israel, when someone dies we sit shivah — observe 7 days of mourning — and the tefillin are wrapped 7 times around the arm. According to the Maharal of Prague, the number 7 represents a complete unit within nature. The Hebrew word for 7 is *sheva*, which is based on the root word *savei'a*, meaning "full" or "satisfied."

The number 8 is one number beyond a complete unit. It enters the world beyond the natural. That is why all the applications of the number 8 in Judaism have to do with supranatural matters: 8 days of Chanukah, commemorating that the tiny amount of oil in the menorah burned for 8 days; 8 garments worn by the high priest. Similarly, a baby boy enters into the covenant of the Jewish people on the eighth day, which represents the day beyond nature, the supranatural.

The Age of Education: When Jewish children, both boys and girls, reach the age of education at three or four, their parents formally begin to teach them Hebrew as well as the laws, traditions, songs, and practical values of Judaism. Small children who attend a Jewish kindergarten, called a *gan* — literally, a garden — are trained in the practices they will perform when they one day become mothers and fathers themselves. On Friday mornings, the children act out the Friday night Shabbos ceremony that their families will perform in their homes later that Friday evening after sundown. One child is chosen as the *ima*, the mother, and lights the Shabbos candles. One child is chosen as the *abba*, the father, and recites the Kiddush, the blessings over the wine (in this case, the grape juice), which sanctify the Sabbath. And some children are chosen to act — as the children.

Passover: The Passover Seder is itself a night of transmission when parents convey to their children the story of the Exodus from Egypt, when we became a nation. The most powerful moment of the night is when the youngest child in the family gets up on a chair and asks the *Mah Nishtanah*, the four questions. This three- or four-year-old child asks his parents: "Why is this night different from all other nights?" "Why do we eat unleavened bread?" "Why do we eat bitter herbs?" "Why do we recline as free men do?" The child asks these questions because he or she wants to be part of the transmission of Judaism. It is a moment of the highest *nachas*, delight, to the parents and grandparents that their offspring want to be the next link in the chain of transmission. And this moment reenacts the moment of freedom when we sat at a family meal in Egypt some three thousand years ago. It is as a family that we reconnect with the birth of the nation. The transmission of values happens in the context of family, one generation to the next.

Bar and Bas Mitzvah: The bar mitzvah and bas mitzvah ceremonies — for a boy at age thirteen and for a girl at age twelve — mark the moment the youth becomes responsible for performing the Torah's 613 commandments. The father symbolically hands the ball to his thirteen-year-old son when, upon the boy's being called to the Torah for the first time, he puts his hand on his son's shoulder and says, "Blessed is the One who has absolved me from the responsibility of bearing this boy's spiritual mistakes."

Until that moment of transmission, the father was responsible for teaching his son, and if the father didn't teach him well and the child made a mistake in following the tradition, the onus of responsibility lay upon the father's shoulders. When a boy turns thirteen, he assumes responsibility for his own mistakes, because he is considered to have matured sufficiently to think things through on his own and to take responsibility for his own actions. The father is absolved from the mistakes of the son; the boy becomes a man. The ball is now in his hands.

When a Jewish girl turns twelve she takes upon herself the obligations of mitzvah observance. She becomes responsible for performing all of the commandments that are incumbent upon a Jewish woman. She has the obligation and joy of observing Shabbos and the Jewish holidays, keeping the kosher dietary laws, praying, learning Torah commandments that apply to women, giving charity, doing acts of *chesed*, not speaking *lashon hara* (evil speech and gossip), and performing all the commandments that are not time bound. She enters into the faith community with the responsibility to grow in character and values as she becomes obligated to the system of personal growth that we call Judaism.

Marriage: The highlight of all transmission moments is the chuppah, the wedding canopy. The years of raising their offspring from birth through childhood and adolescence culminate in this moment when parents escort their child to the marriage canopy. As they walk their child down the aisle, the parents enter into a new dimension of time, space, and soul — they taste eternity. In that moment, as they look at each other over the head of their child, the parents experience Jewish continuity itself. And they are the conduits of that continuity as they lead their child to their first Jewish home, the chuppah.

This chuppah is a piece of cloth representing the roof of the couple's new home, held up by four poles, representing the four walls. The four walls are open to the elements, representing the open kindness that will emanate from this home. Just as Abraham and Sarah's tent was open on four sides so that they could welcome guests from north, south, east, and west, so, too, this new Jewish couple establishes their home based on these principles of *chesed* and the welcoming of guests.

Home Run Tips 🏏

The couple and their parents stand under the chuppah, which represents the establishment of a new Jewish home in the Jewish community. It is a public declaration that the parents have succeeded in integrating within the minds of their children the willingness to take their own place as the transmitters of Torah values in a new home dedicated to the living of those values. When your children, of their own free will, decide to follow in your footsteps and establish a home based on the values, ethics, and laws of Judaism, you have won the World Series — you have won the game of life.